The Book of Festivals and Holidays the World Over

Marguerite Ickis

With drawings by Richard E. Howard

DODD, MEAD & COMPANY   NEW YORK

Grateful acknowledgement is made to the following
for use of the material indicated:

Friendship Press:
Two festivals, the New Year Festival (San Khuda)
and the Old New Year (Ana Viejo)
from *Children's Festivals from Many Lands.*

INTRODUCTION

Festivals are flourishing all over the world because more people are taking advantage of increasingly economical, improved transportation and longer vacations. The European Travel Commission and travel agencies have cooperated to promote tourism by making it possible for people to visit festivals in out-of-the-way places and at off seasons. Many vacationers go abroad to satisfy their curiosity about life and customs in other countries. Probably the best time to see the most people is during a festival which reflects the culture of the region in which it takes place, its economic and recreational attractions, and the ethnic beliefs of the citizens.

There are movable holidays and festivals that fall on different days in different years. Many are rural in nature and take place according to the four seasons: winter, spring, summer, and fall; but this does not mean that they are celebrated at the same time everywhere—when it is springtime in South America, it is autumn in the North. Religious festivals dot the calendars in every country and are observed according to the birth or martrydom of their religious leaders. But there are other factors that make it almost impossible for the layman to determine the date of holidays celebrated by religious orders. Jewish people, for instance, begin the religious year in the Hebrew month of Tishri, which is the month of September. People in Asia and Africa measure the year by movements of the moon. Their holidays are known as *lunar* holidays, and they have a calendar with thirteen months instead of twelve. In this book, we have placed the holidays and festivals,

v

to the best of our ability, in chronological order according to the United States calendar that begins in January and ends in December.

It is always desirable to revive and record entertainment of the past with a purpose in mind. For example, today the Middle East and Far East are front-page news, and for this reason, we have explored in depth some of their important festivals in order to give meaning to their customs and entertainment. It is hoped that children everywhere will enjoy the charming stories related to these celebrations. We have also endeavored to select material that can be adapted to group activities such as fairs, special days, or plays that might be international or interfaith.

In this book we have selected only holidays and festivals that are current and give promise of continuing indefinitely. Some world festivals have been omitted—this is because they have already been recorded (including traditional music, dances, games, and entertainment in previous books by the author, namely, *The Book of Patriotic Holidays, The Book of Festival Holidays, The Book of Religious Holidays* and *The Book of Games and Entertainment the World Over.*

CONTENTS

INTRODUCTION   V

1. NEW YEAR'S AROUND THE WORLD   1
   United States — Europe — Germany — Greece — New Year's Food
   — New Year's in the Middle East, Rosh Hashana and Yom Kippur
   — Iran, *Nu-Ruz* — India — New Year's in the Far East, China —
   Yuan Shaw, Festival of Lanterns — Thailand — Vietnam, *Tet
   Nguyen Dan* — Birthdays, Vietnam — Japan, *Oshoogatsu* — Africa
   — South America, Old Year, Ecuador — Brazil — Bolivia — Mexico
   Cross of Petition — The New Year of Trees

2. EPIPHANY—JANUARY 6   19
   Epiphany Celebrations, United States — Europe — Germany —
   Spain — Greek Orthodox, Blessing of the Waters — Greece —
   Middle East — "Night of Destiny" — Two Eastern Legends

3. WINTER FESTIVALS   25
   China, Star Festival — Hawaii, Narcissus Festival — Japan, Read-
   ing Poems at the Imperial Palace — Candlemas — Groundhog Day
   — Valentine's Day — Alaska, Iceworm "Winter Wonderland" Fes-
   tival — Carnival — United States, Mardi Gras — Carnivals in
   Europe, France — Belgium — Spain and Portugal — Italy — Greece
   — Virgin Islands — Mexico — South America, Peru, Water-Throw-
   ing Carnival — Peru, Finishing of the House — Peru, Baby's First
   Haircut — Brazil — Purim — Shrove Tuesday

4. LENT   45
   Ancient Lenten Calendars — Ash Wednesday — World Day of
   Prayer — Mothering Sunday — Laetare Sunday — Palm Sunday —
   Palm Sunday in Rome

5. HOLY WEEK   51

Greek Orthodox Holy Week — Good Friday — Good Friday in Spain — Holy Saturday — Greek Orthodox Easter — Protestant Churches

6. EASTER   58

Sunrise Services — The Easter Parade — The Easter Rabbit — Easter Eggs — Easter Foods — Easter in Africa — Lapp Lady Day

7. EARLY SPRING FESTIVALS   63

Observance of Passover — Whitsuntide — Corpus Christi — Corpus Christi, in the United States — Corpus Christi in Europe — Corpus Christi in Mexico — Shavuot — Procession of the Swallow — Doll Festival — Russia, International Women's day — St. Patrick's Day — Egypt, The Smelling of Spring — Marshal Tito's Birthday — All Fool's Day — Shellfish Gathering — Birth of Buddha, in Japan — In China — Birthday of Mohammed — Five Principal Islam Holidays — Turkey, Children's Day — St. George's Day

8. LATE SPRING FESTIVALS   84

May Day Celebrations — Singing in the May — Hanging May Baskets — Tree Planting Ceremonies — Birthday Trees — Alm Tree — Ching Ming — Blossom Festivals — United States, Shenandoah Valley — United States, Wenatchee Valley — Canada, Annapolis Valley — Japan, Cherry Viewing — Holland, Tulip Festival — China, Spring Ox — India, Masi Magham — Japan, Kite Flying — Mexico, Day of Holy Cross — United States, Bird Week — Japan — Cormorant Fishing — Purple Spring in Peru

9. SUMMER FESTIVALS   97

Japan, Time-Observance Day — St. John's Day — Estonia, Singing Festival — Scandinavian Countries — Greece — Canada — Mexico — Denmark — Brazil — St. Peter's Day — Dragon Boat Festival — Belgium, Shrimp Festival — Japan, Night-Singing Insects — Italy, The Cricket — Switzerland, First Fruits of the Alps — India, Gayatri Japam — Hindu, Avani Mulam — Assumption Day — Japan, Climbing Mt. Fuji — Peru, Promenades of Santo Domingo and San Francisco

10. FALL FESTIVALS   112

Fast of Ramadan — End of Fast — Elevation of the Cross — Sticky-Sticky Fair — Book Reading Week — Eighth Moon Festivals, Festival of Reunion — Worship of the Moon — Moon Cakes — Moon

Hare — Kite Day in China — Harvest Festivals — All Hallow's Eve — Guy Fawkes Day — Wine Festival on St. Martin's Day — St. Martin Festival in Germany — Ceremonies in Africa — Blessing of the Spears — Fisherman's Prayer — Sukkot — St. Mênas' Day — Thanksgiving — Hurricane Thanksgiving — Thanksgiving for Birds

11. ADVENT   127
    Star of Seven — Santon Fair — Christmas Market in Nuremberg — St. Nicholas Day — Greece — Feast of Immaculate Conception Philippine Islands — Music for Our Lady — Day of Ste Lucia, Sweden — Italy — Hanukkah

12. CHRISTMAS THE WORLD OVER   135
    The Giving of Gifts — Christmas in the United States — Europe, Northern Countries — Church Service — Yule Men — Decorations — Christmas Trees — Cookies — Food for Birds and Animals — Christmas Customs — Eastern Europe — Switzerland — Southern Europe — The Three Mass — Christmas Crib — Réveillon — Christmas Celebrations — Christmas in the Middle East — Christmas in Africa — Christmas in the Far East — Central America — South America

    INDEX   159

THE BOOK OF
FESTIVALS AND HOLIDAYS
THE WORLD OVER

1. NEW YEAR'S AROUND THE WORLD

Welcoming the New Year is one of the oldest customs the world over, but not every country celebrates it on the same date. In the Near East and parts of Asia the New Year is supposed to begin when winter gives place to the beauties of spring. The Chinese and Vietnamese celebrate their New Year according to the first day of the month in the lunar calendar, which falls sometime between January 21 and February 19. Jews all over the world celebrate Rosh Hashana (Yom Kippur) at the end of the summer, close to the autumn equinox. In India, the Hindus celebrate the first day of each season, so they have four New Years on their calendar. The date on which the American and European countries celebrate New Year's (January 1) is inherited from the Romans. It was Julius Caesar who changed the date from March to January in honor of Janus Befors, a god with two faces. One face always looked back to the old year and the other looked forward to the new.

In every country New Year's provides an occasion for a new beginning. To the Jew, the day is sometimes called "Day of the Sounding of the Ram's Horn"—the call from the Heavenly Shepherd to listen to the voice of God. On this day the Book of Life is opened, and good and evil acts, words and thoughts of each

1

person, are examined. To many people New Year's Day provides an ocasion for closing rifts and healing disputes; as much as anything else it is a day of reconciliation. Today, the spirit of the New Year, everywhere, is to make the coming year better than the year that has just passed into eternity.

The custom of making noise to welcome the New Year goes back to the ancient practice of driving evil spirits away from the house. In Denmark young people "smash in the New Year" by banging on their friends' doors and throwing bits of broken pottery (collected during the year) against the sides of houses. Japanese dancers go from house to house making weird noises by rattling bamboo sticks and pounding drums. In Vietnam, salvos of firecrackers mark the ceremony of welcoming the New Year, and most South American countries "let the New Year in" by setting off fireworks.

UNITED STATES

It is customary for most Americans to stay up until midnight on New Year's Eve to enjoy the magic moment when one year gives place to another. Church bells ring out, horns toot, whistles blow, and everyone is noisy and gay. But the leisurely old custom of receiving friends, dispensing cheer, or making holiday calls on New Year's Day has declined. Instead, the television is turned on with the morning coffee and the first of the bowl parades is in progress. Before the day is ended, the football fan will have watched scrimmages that take place in the Sugar Bowl in New Orleans, Louisiana, the Cotton Bowl in Dallas, Texas, the Rose Bowl in Pasadena, California, or the Orange Bowl in Miami, Florida. The parades in between are colorful, relaxing spectacles, and the Tournament of Roses parade seems each year to be more elaborate and sophisticated. A football fan won't complain that the bowl games and television in combination have changed the nation's New Year's habits, but others, no doubt, would prefer visiting with friends.

EUROPE

In European countries, especially in Denmark, Norway, Italy, and Portugal, a family starts the New Year by first attending church. Sometimes the service will take the form of Holy Communion and the people make vows regarding the New Year. The tradition of "First Footing," based on the belief that the character of the first person entering the household after midnight affects its welfare, is still very real in most European countries. It is always planned that a fair person should enter first—a good omen for the coming year. On New Year's Day friends go calling, bearing gifts of cake, bread and cheese, and in turn, the host has to offer a hot pint or a bottle of wine. Each drinks "A good health and Happy New Year" and more good wishes for the day.

GERMANY

German people believe one should live the first day of the New Year the way it should be lived every day during the coming twelve months. Among other things, the hausfrau spends extra time making her house spotless, and the whole family wear their best clothes. In certain communities the night watchman still goes about at midnight on New Year's Eve and recites the traditional verse:

3

In the name of the Lord
The old Year goes out the door.
This is my wish for each of you:
Praise to God, our Lord.

In Oberammergau, a "star singer," carrying a large illuminated star on a long pole, leads the villagers and visitors on New Year's Eve in a procession that last several hours. His song reviews the events of the past year and extends good wishes for the one to come. In this Passion Play village an entire band—selected members of the Passion Play Orchestra—marches with the procession. Magnificent voices are heard, and many a marcher can be recognized as from the Oberammergau stage or choir.

At the same time, the costumed youth of Oberammergau are on the march with the "little star," accompanied by a small orchestra: a few violins, a bass viol, and a guitar.

GREECE

New Year's Day acquires special significance in Greece from the fact, on this day, reverence is done to the memory of one of the greatest fathers of the Greek Orthodox Church, St. Basil. He becomes the bearer, and donor, of blessings that anyone standing at the opening of the year expects and hopes for—wealth and prosperity.

On New Year's Eve not only children but grownups go from house to house singing the *kalanda*. In their hands each carries an apple, a paper ship, or a paper star, and usually a green rod

from a cornel or some other tree. With this branch they tap the master of the home and his family on the back, while they sing their good wishes. The housewife always gives the children something, usually a coin which they stick into the side of their orange or apple.

In rural communities it is the custom to bring a stone or sand into the house. The heaviness of the stone, the number of moss patches on it, the number of grains of sand are all so many guarantees that the crops will be good during the coming year. Thus, when visiting a neighbor or relative on New Year's Day, one must bring a mossy stone into the house and throw it down saying: "May the purse of the master of the house grow as heavy as this stone." All stones brought into the house by visiting friends and relations are gathered into a heap and thrown away after eight days. Sometimes the stone is so large that the guest has to carry it on his back; this is considered good luck for the master of the house.

New Year's Food

In almost every country the pig has always been a symbol of good luck, so pork, or a suckling pig, is a favored food for a New Year's dinner. It has been said that this custom arose because a pig roots in a *forward* direction, this being a symbol of a "fat future." By the same token, anyone partaking of turkey, goose, or other fowl on that day will not prosper throughout the year. The reason? Because all fowl scratch *backward* in searching for food.

It is the custom in Spain and Portugal to select twelve grapes from a bunch on New Year's Eve. Just as the bells strike twelve, each person pops the grapes into his mouth as he offers New Year's wishes. This act is aid to insure twelve happy months in the coming year.

NEW YEAR'S IN THE MIDDLE EAST

Rosh Hashana and Yom Kippur, Jewish New Year

Rosh Hashana marks the beginning of the Jewish New Year, which is celebrated at the end of summer, close to the autumn

5

equinox. It begins the Ten Days of Penitence that culminate in the fasting and in the religious services of Yom Kippur, the Day of Atonement. These High Holy Days are the most solemn of the Jewish religious observances. They are a time set aside for earnest self-judgment by individuals, rather than a joyous celebration.

This season was designed to soften the erring heart of man with contrition for misdeeds, thus leading him to wholehearted repentance by the time Yom Kippur arrived. On Rosh Hashana, services in the synagogues are marked with great solemnity. After an elaborate liturgy, the *Shofar*, the ram's horn, is sounded. Its clarion call is, as it were, a summons to the worshippers to look within, to search their consciences, and then come to sincere repentance. The belief is that nine days hence, on Yom Kippur, the celestial book of accounts will be closed and judgment reached.

In a Jewish home the *kiddush* (the "sanctification prayer") is recited, and the festive lights are kindled on the eve of Rosh

Hashana. A piece of sweet apple is dipped in honey, the person who performs this symbolic act repeats, "May it be God's will to grant us a good and sweet year." On the second night, some kind of fruit is tasted that has not yet been eaten during the year. Then an appropriate benediction is recited.

The *Neilah* is the concluding service on Yom Kippur, when

worshippers make their final peace with god and their conscience. God's book of deeds is closed, and judgment having been reached, is ready to be opened again for another year.

Iran, No-Ruz

No-Ruz, Iran's New Year, begins on March 21 and lasts for thirteen days. This Asian country is unusually dry, swept by cold winds in the winter and intense heat in the summer, so No-Ruz is a joyous occasion because March marks the beginning of spring.

Preparation for the New Year begins several weeks in advance, when the family scatters quick-growing seeds, such as wheat, celery, and lentils, in shallow bowls containing a little earth and water. The custom of growing this type of garden dates back to mythology; when Adonis was out hunting, a boar gored the youth in the thigh and killed him. In his honor, Aphrodite founded a funeral cult which was celebrated each spring by Syrian women, and it then spread throughout the ancient world. Seeds were planted in vases and watered with warm water; these plants sprouted quickly, but died soon, and the vases were known as "Gardens of Adonis."

The Iranians believe that people should be happy when the New Year arrives. Often each member of the family will eat a piece of candy while a passage is being read from the Koran, the Muslim holy book. Then they embrace each other and say, "May you live a hundred years."

At the start of the holiday, rooms are thoroughly cleaned and children receive new clothes and gifts. The evening before No-Ruz begins, a traditional omelet made with greens is eaten with pilaf, the national dish of rice, symbolizing an abundant year. Friends visit and exchange gifts such as colored eggs, fruits, and bunches of narcissus.

The most outstanding feature of the New Year's celebration is a special festival table, which is a cloth spread out on the floor on which are *Haft-sin*, or "Seven S's"—objects, according to the Zoroastrian religion, that represent happiness in the New Year. They are:

7

Sabyeh—green sprouts grown from seed
Sonbul—hyacinth
Samanoo—sweet wheat pudding
Serkeh—vinegar
Sumac—same as our sumac plant
Seeb—apple
Senjed—Bohemian olives.

In addition to the Haft-sin, there are other symbolic objects on the table. These include a colored egg, a mirror, and a candle for each member of the family. The egg and the mirror have an interesting significance. Legend says the earth trembles slightly as it begins the New Year. At the precise moment, an egg is placed on the mirror. To everyone's intense delight the egg always trembles a bit—perhaps due to the rumble and vibrations of cannons that go off at the same instant to proclaim the arrival of the New Year. After a feast which includes roast chicken, fruits, bread, and sweets is over, a passage from the Koran is read.

On the thirteenth day of No-Ruz, called *Sizdar-Bedah*, or Thirteenth Day Out," it is considered unlucky to stay in the house. The entire family goes to the country to enjoy the spring, and perhaps a picnic lunch. The children gather up the Adonis Gardens and on their way carefully throw them into a stream of running water. This symbolizes the throwing away of bad luck, family quarrels, and illness.

INDIA

Holi or *Basaat*, a Hindu New Year, is celebrated sometime in April or May. It is also known as the "Fire Festival" because boys and girls alike have water pistols filled with saffron- and crimson-colored water which they squirt over each other and people on the street. The festival takes place just before the rainstorms that come each year, so water is a most symbolic theme for the festival.

People of India believe that bathing in the Ganges and other sacred waters will protect them from evil. Women and girls bathe early in the morning and don colorful saris for the day. The entire family goes to one of the beautiful temples to listen to the reading of the calendar for the New Year, after which there is an elaborate feast and exchange of gifts.

Maharram, a Muslim New Year, is a festival held to honor members of Muslim orders who take vows of poverty and austerity and live in monasteries. These holy men are called "dervishes." The main feature of the holiday is the skilled dances performed by men and boys alone. Little boys who take part in the ceremony are dressed as holy men and go about begging for alms to support the various orders.

NEW YEAR'S IN THE FAR EAST

China

Yuan Tan, the Chinese New Year, is celebrated on the first day of the month in lunar calendar and lasts for fourteen days. People who view television are familiar with the dragon that goes up and down the street on the last night of the festival, demanding alms or to be destroyed. He has a large papier-mâché head to which is fastened a long red velvet train ornamented with embroidery and jewel-like sparklers. However, the most beautiful and specatcular event—the Festival of Lanterns—has never been seen in all its splendor outside China itself.

Yaun Shaw, Festival of Lanterns

Yuan Shaw, Festival of Lanterns, is celebrated on the night of the full moon during the Chinese New Years. The Republic of China recognizes the feast by closing public offices, by street declarations, and by displays of fireworks called "the letting off of flowers" in public parks. In old China the Feast of Lanterns was regarded as preeminently a holiday season for children. During several days before and after the full moon, which is the fifteenth day of the festival, bands of young village boys dress up in strange garments and go about by day and night acting queer plays, partly in dumb shows, partly in speech, dance, and song. At night they carry large lighted lanterns and march amid music and song

9

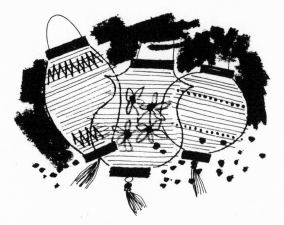

through the streets of their native village, or from one village to another, stopping occasionally in front of a prominent villager's house to act their little play or perform a lantern dance.

In Peking, the lantern festival no doubt is less brilliant than of old. Gone are the days when the lantern show in the capital included works of art by well-known artists, worth a thousand ounces of silver! The shops of Lantern Street outside the Ch'ien Mên had a glittering exhibition as an advertisement to attract purchasers. The varieties displayed were infinite and, just for the record, let us mention a few.

Wall lanterns to put on either side of the front door were offered in pairs. Others were sold in sets, eight or sixteen, intended to be hung together and thus form a complete picture; "Guest Lanterns," large white silk moons decorated with the purchaser's name and lucky bats, intended to light visitors across the courtyard to the reception hall, stood ready on bamboo poles. Cheap paper lanterns, cunningly made to copy living creatures, hung from the ceiling; fantastic crabs with moving claws, dragon flies with flapping wings, birds with swaying necks. Glass or gauze panels painted with historic scenes, mounted in carved wood frames, were displayed in many varieties. Inside the shops there were many special lanterns for many special occasions. Of such were ones in the shape of little boys, intended for presents to childless families; "heavenly lanterns" to be hoisted on a high pole in the courtyard and decorated with fir branches; round toy-lanterns made to roll on the ground like a fireball; lanterns set on wheels; red paper lamps pricked with tiny pinholes to form a lucky character, such as "happiness" or "prosperity"; or horse-racing lanterns which consisted of two or more wire frames, one within the other, arranged on the principle of the smokejack so that a current of air sets them revolving; and, finally, crossword-puzzle lanterns, with riddles pasted on their sides, intended to hang outside a scholar's home for the amusement of his literary friends.

Thailand

Songkran is a Buddhist New Year's festival that is celebrated April 15 and lasts three days. It is sometimes called "Water Festival" because the main entertainment is to throw water on one another. Everyone carries buckets or bowls for scooping up the water, and mock battles follow, especially among groups of children. The Thai people believe that there is great merit in acts of kindness, so before the holiday children buy birds in order to set them free on Songkran. Also, girls in gay dresses carry fish bowls down to the river and throw the fish back. A water-festival queen is chosen and paraded along the streets with bands playing amid laughter and the sound of splashing water.

Pee-Mai. This Thailand New Year's festival is celebrated by grownups in honor of Buddha's birthday. Men and boys pull a gay pagoda, decorated with paper flags, through the streets, and following close behind is an enormous hollow log with a "fire" inside. Boys beat drums and others strike gongs as the procession moves along.

In the meantime, other processions are taking place in different parts of the city. They include all kinds of images—green dragons, blue buffaloes, elephants, huge men—and all meet simultaneously at the Buddha temple. Buddha has been draped in a new yellow robe for the hot season, and people go into the temple and bow to his image. The women douse the image with water, a symbol of purification. Everyone lights a taper and places it on the altar, together with their offering. Then all go outside for a feast.

11

The ceremony ends with *water throwing* when people go about carrying silver bowls of scented water. When they greet friends, they throw the scented water at them. Soon everyone is soaked and having a happy time.

Vietnam
Tet Nguyen Dan, Vietnam New Year

The Tet, or Vietnamese New Year, is the most important celebration in Vietnam and certainly the most publicized in American newspapers and television. It is considered the most religious, attractive, and picturesque festival, not only in Saigon, but in Hanoi as well.

The solemnities begin days prior to Tet, which commences the first day of the first month of the lunar year. The warmest and liveliest of colors are displayed in shop windows, in house interiors, and in the new clothes made for the occasion. On this holiday people of all classes spend their money for purchases of the most extravagant items in order to greet the New Year properly.

The head of the family lights candles on the ancestral altar, and trayloads of delicacies and paper articles portraying a heron, a horse, a pair of high boots, and a courtier's robe are offered to the household gods. This is the ceremony "bidding farewell to the kitchen gods," who are supposed to ascend to heaven to present their report on members of the family of which they are the guardians. Exploding firecrackers mark their departure for the heavens, which is at the time of the family meal, composed of dishes taken from the family altar.

The last day before Tet, from noon on, the streets are empty of people and markets are closed. The members of the family take turns bowing in front of the altar, three times each, and saying a formula of welcome to the ancestral spirits. At exactly midnight the spirits return, and from this moment all human problems and worries are set aside. The sound of firecrackers and gunshots mark the welcome ceremony, which continues until dawn.

All the words and actions on this first morning are to be carefully checked, because they may be omens; superstition reigns supreme. Everybody lies in wait for the first animal cry to be heard. Will it be a cock? If so, it portends bad crops, because the fowl will eat all the grain! Or a buffalo? There will be a toilsome year ahead! If a dog's bark is heard, there will be no fear of theft.

Social calls on New Year's Day are rare, because the personality of the visitor influences the fate of the visited family for the next 365 days. Certain families take the precaution of closing their homes to unexpected guests and solicit instead the visit of a prominent person who will assure them good luck.

It is forbidden to squabble with one another during the first days of the New Year, and there may be no words of anger or coarse language. The offerings to the ancestors go on, and each trade has its own cult—the laborer pays a pious tribute to his plow, the craftsman to his tools. Protecting gods of these instruments receive offerings of flowers and incense, alcohol and meals.

At dusk on the third day of the festival, the families bid farewell to the spirits of their ancestors. To make the separation, much votive paper is burned, to symbolize the gold and silver that will be needed on the long journey to the other world.

On the seventh day the bamboo pole is removed from the yard, the people return to their daily lives and normal occupations, free of any dreams. However, the Tet is not over, the festival will continue informally until their resources are completely expended.

Birthdays, Vietnam

When a child is born in Vietnam, his horoscope is cast immediately. The chart shows the hour of birth, the day, the month of the year, and where the planets are in the heavens at the moment. From this information, the astrologer predicts how the movements of the planets will effect the child's life. An infant born in this country is usually assigned a lucky-hour symbol. For example, if he is born between five o'clock and seven o'clock in the morning, his lucky symbol is a cat.

Japan
Oshoogatsu, New Year

The Japanese people attach great importance to the beginning and end of all events; thus the year end and the New Year season are momentous occasions for them. To satisfy their old-time custom, December is the month to settle all outstanding debts in order to start the new year with a clean slate. As in almost every country, housecleaning is most important and must be completed before New Year's Day, and new clothes are provided for the family.

The pine, bamboo, and rice-straw rope are the New Year's decorations of outstanding importance. Beside the front door, branches of pine are hung because it is said that, of all evergreens, the pine is the most enduring, retaining it's deep green under all weather conditions. It is also indicative of health and strength and is regarded as a spirit of longevity.

Bamboo stalks are also hung. They grow straight and fast, representing a symbol of uprightness and rapid development. A sacred rice-straw rope, called *Shimekazari*, is considered the most important of the New Year's decorations and is hung over the front and back doors, the barn door, around the well, and up over the roof to sanctify the home. It is a long brushlike arrangement of straw to which objects signifying happiness and good luck are attached. These include seaweed, fern, a red-and-white paper fan on which is written the Japanese character meaning "to celebrate happy events."

On New Year's Eve adults stay up for the night-watch gong. It rings 108 times to purge the 108 weaknesses described by

14

Buddha's teaching. The New Year is officially opened by the Imperial Household of Japan at the Imperial Sanctuary with the *shinkhohai*, or "worshipping in the four directions." The Emperor prays for divine blessing for the country and for peace and plenty during the year.

Early in the morning members of the family place pink-and-white rice cakes and many kinds of fruit before the ancestral tablets and family shrine. A family meal follows, after which the Japanese go to visit their friends and relations and toast each other with "May your New Year be happy." The shops and businesses are closed, and few people are on the streets the first three days of the New Year.

AFRICA

In the Mandigo tribe of Sierra Leone, the New Year's festival comes at the seed-sowing time in late April or early May and lasts a day and a half. This is the end of the dry season, when temperatures have evaporated the water from the streams and rivers, scorched the grass, and stopped most plant growth. The ensuing wet season bring the flowing of the rivers, the growing of plants and greenness of grass, generally renewing life. For centuries the people have believed that water is the source of life and that it loses its power through use. Hence, they believe that an act of God takes the old water away as the old year ends and that this miracle occurs at sunset of the last day of the closing year. Therefore the people must give thanks and rejoice.

The festival is enjoyed by young and old alike. On New Year's Eve the houses are cleaned, yards are swept, and troughs and utensils are made ready to receive the new water. Mothers and children gather in the village square and begin singing and dancing to the accompaniment of drums and flutes. At the spring, buckets are filled with water and carried to town on the heads of the celebrants. After this they return to the spring in family groups to bring water needed for each household. Some of the children go back and forth three times to get the water required.

15

Old Year, Ecuador

The whole family enters into the plans and preparation for the thrilling celebration of Old Year, Año Viejo, held in Ecuador on December 31. One member will donate an old shirt, another a pair of pants, another a hat. These are stuffed with straw and sewed together to represent the Old Year. Sometimes cypress branches are gathered into an arch over the figure's chair, which is set up outdoors in front of the house, A pipe may go into his mouth, a cane in his hand. There the old man will sit while the children dance gaily about him. Inside the house someone will write his last will and testament, usually listing family faults that must go off with the old year. At midnight, or before, if there are little ones that must go to bed early, the will of the old man is read aloud before the whole family with much laughing and joking. Then a match is lit, and the old man goes up in flames, taking the family faults with him.

Often someone will dress in black as the old man's widow and go around to the others begging for charity. At midnight the streets are filled with burning men and begging widows. After this ceremony comes the eating of the spiced food prepared for the occasion. The typical New Year's dish is a crisp fried pastry

16

in the shape of a doughnut, which is dipped after cooking into a brown sugar syrup.

Brazil

On New Year's Eve in Rio de Janiero, Copacabana beach glows with thousands of candles placed on the sand in homage to the sea queen. It is the custom for women to dress in long white robes and wade into the water to strew petals in the thundering surf.

Bolivia

Alacitas, which is one of Bolivia's oldest festivals, is celebrated early in January. It is of Indian origin and the theme of the celebration has to do with "Ereko," the god of abundance. He is depicted as a little man, and thousands of Ekeko dolls and figures are made of wood or straw and sold in the markets for New Year's. The dolls are decorated with pots and pans, food and clothing, and sometimes coins, and all objects are made as realistic as possible. It is customary to hang the dolls just outside the door as guardian of the home. Since Ekeko is considered the god of good luck, the articles he is wearing will surely come to the household sometime during the year.

Mexico

New Year's in Mexico is much the same as the United States. Most newly elected officials take office January 1, which is an occasion for a feast with special foods, drinks, and sometimes folk dancing.

Cross of Petition

On New Year's Day many Mexicans make a pilgrimage to Milla Oaxoca to present their wishes before a Cross of Petition. First, they pray at the cross, make an offering of flowers, candles, and incense, which they blow in four directions.

The people make miniature models of the things they desire and place them at the foot of the cross. Everything is made to scale and with great care. Houses are made of split cane; burros

17

and cattle are represented by erect sticks, pigs by heaps of stone inside a corral formed of larger stones. Cornfields are laid out with furrows and straw to represent the corn, bags of soil as the grain; yellow berries suggest oranges, grapefruits, and lemons.

HAMISH ASAR BISHVAT, THE NEW YEAR OF TREES

On the fifteenth day of the Hebrew month of Shavat, which falls in January or February, Jewish children all over the world observe Hamish Asar Bishvat, the New Year of Trees.

The festival began in ancient Palestine when it was the custom for a father to plant a cedar sapling for a male child born during the year and a cypress for a female child. At marriage the respective trees would be cut down and used as posts for the traditional wedding canopy. But during the many centuries when Jews were away from Palestine, the trees were destroyed, and no new ones were planted so that the once fertile land became a desolate desert.

Thus, in present-day Israel, Hamish Asar Bishvat has become a day of planting trees to provide such fruits as pomegranates, almonds, dates, figs, oranges, lemons, and grapefruit, and also to restore beauty to the countryside. The children are given the opportunity of doing the planting, and the ceremony is followed by cheerful parties.

Since Hamish Asah Bishvat falls in January or February, during the winter season, Jewish children in the United States and Europe observe the holiday in a different way. On this holiday, they partake of a variety of Israeli fruits, and Hebrew lessons are devoted to a study of Israel's geography and agricultural products.

2. EPIPHANY, JANUARY 6

As a feast day, Epiphany, or Twelfth Night, stands high in importance on the Christian calendar in countries along the Mediterranean Sea. In northern European countries, it is sometimes called "Feast of the Three Kings," as it celebrates the Three Wise Men who, led by a bright star in the sky, came to Bethlehem twelve days after the birth of Christ. January 6 has been a feast day in Egypt for centuries. On this date Egyptians celebrate their winter solstice festival in honor of the Nile River. Therefore it is natural that in this part of the world Epiphany symbolizes the baptism of Christ in the Jordan River, rather than the Western tradition of the Adoration of the Magi.

The word "Epiphany" comes from the Greek word meaning "appearance" or "manifestation of the Son of God to man. The Eastern churches hold that the Epiphany celebrates Christ's baptism by St. John and also two other events—the miracle at Cana in turning water into wine and the feeding of the five thousand—both of which are said to have occurred on this date.

In every country, East and West, the Magi are accepted as wise men famous for their knowledge of natural sciences, including astrology and astronomy. The Magi carefully observed the stars and on the night of Christ's birth it is said they noticed a star shining in the west more brilliantly than any star ever shone before. They determined to follow it, and when it stood still over Bethlehem, they found the Christ Child in a manger.

It has never been definitely determined from which country the Magi came, or how many there were on the trip to Bethlehem. An old tradition of the Oriental church says there were twelve. However, the Western church established the belief, which has come down to us, that there were three "Magi," or "kings."

The first to arrive was an Ethiopian. He was middle-aged, dark-skinned, and thick-lipped, with a short dark beard. His name was Balthasar and he was wearing an Egyptian costume. The myrrh he held in his hands prefigured the death of the Son of God.

The second was a Hindu, an old man with a long beard, and some say he represented old age. His name was Melchior. He brought gold in testimony of Christ's royalty.

The third, a Greek, was young, representing the *future*. He was blue-eyed, beardless, and his name was Gaspar. His gift of frankincense was a token of the child's divinity.

EPIPHANY CELEBRATIONS

United States

Epiphany in America is celebrated mostly by religious groups. To children, January 6 means Twelfth Night, or the anniversary of the night the Three Wise Men were guided to Bethlehem by a blazing star in the winter sky. In churches and homes all over the United States, we find the Christmas crib constructed with loving care as a part of the holiday decoration or center of special religious ceremonies. Over the centuries many variations have been added to the crèche, but always there is the central group— the Babe in the manger, Mary and Joseph, the shepherds, and the Three Wise Men. In Catholic churches, the Christmas drama is terminated on Epiphany Eve, or Twelfth Night, with the altaring of the crib. Another star is placed over it and the three Magi take the place of shepherds. They are usually depicted as kings mounted on camels; in their hands are the traditional gifts of gold, frankincense, and myrrh.

Europe

In many European countries special ceremonies are held on January 6 in honor of the Three Magi. In Sweden, Austria, and Switzerland, for example, young people choose three among them to dress in costumes of the three kings. Then, following the kings, they form processions through the streets of the villages, singing special carols and carrying a large "Star of Bethlehem" as their banner.

Germany

Christmas carols are so numerous in all European countries, they can be grouped under many headings, according to subject. The largest category is the Nativity carols, followed by the star carols, usually associated with the Magi. A charming "star" ceremony, typical of others, takes place in the Alps on Epiphany.

In the Bavarian Alps there is a beautiful custom that is followed on Epiphany Eve in many small mountain villages. A group is headed by a man carrying on a long pole the "great star," beautifully lighted from within. On it, little Jesus and other religious motifs are painted in color. Behind the star carrier march the "star singers," followed by the entire village. At all important buildings and squares in the village they stop and sing the old star carols, melodies and words sometimes dating back to the sixteenth century.

Spain

According to an old Spanish tradition, the Magi are said to journey to Bethlehem every year. And so, on Epiphany Eve, the children are laden with gifts as they wait at the city gates to meet the kings. They look for the group in the sunset, but soon the glorious vision fades and the children turn homeward, believing the kings to have passed behind the mountains.

The "Blessing of the Waters" first takes place on the eve of Epiphany in the church. After the service, the priest goes around the village with the Cross, visiting each home in order to bless it. All rooms are sprinkled with a sprig of basil dipped in holy water. In many villages, the procession goes from house to house, singing the kalanda of the Eve of Epiphany. This is their customary song: "Epiphany has come, illumination of the world, and great rejoicing in the Lord. By Jordan River stands our good Mary, and thus she begs St. John the Baptist, it is in your power to baptize the child of God."

The second and most important blessing of the waters takes place on the day of Epiphany itself, January 6. Then the Cross is thrown into the sea or reservoir with great pomp and ceremony. The golden church banners head the procession, and the priests following are dressed in their finest robes. In larger towns and cities, this ritual takes on an official character and is attended by state authorities, aldermen, and military bands. As soon as the priest throws the Cross into the water, a number of young men dive for it. The one who brings it to the surface has the privilege of carrying it around the town and is presented with gifts from the people of the place.

Greece

The Greeks are a seafaring people; thus it is natural that they should attach particular importance to the blessing of the waters. Not so long ago, when ships still sailed under canvas, most seamen tried to be home before Christmas, believing it was not good to be at sea during the Twelve Days. They cast anchor and waited for the waters to be blessed before venturing upon their next journey. Even today, when the invention of steam enables ships to be at sea in all kinds of weather, Greek seamen try to be back in their home ports for Epiphany. All craft lying in the harbor on the day of Epiphany, from the largest passenger-ship to the smallest rowboat, are decked with bunting. The moment the Cross is thrown into the water, the church bells begin ringing, while steamships sound their whistles, and the warships fire off their cannons.

Middle East

As the name "Epiphany" implies, the Festival of the Nativity was Eastern in origin, rather than Western. On this day, January 6, the water in the Nile River was supposed to be purest and so was stored in special containers for use on holy occasions throughout the year. With the arrival of Christianity in Egypt, the day was celebrated as the anniversary of Christ's baptism in the river Jordan, and holy water is still drawn from the Nile and used for the year's baptisms and sacraments. This custom spread as far east as Nigeria, where a feast called *Timkat* celebrates the day Christ was baptized by St. John. There is a procession of priests, followed by devout worshippers who go to a spring or pool for the ceremony. A priest dressed in a splendid rope dips up some of the water, blesses it, and then sprinkles the pilgrims with it.

Lailat-al-Quade, "Night of Destiny"

In Arab countries, Christians have a festival called *Lailat-al-Quade*, which means "Night of Destiny." It is celebrated on Epiphany Eve, which is considered to be the anniversary of Christ's baptism. During the day children visit banks of streams and rivers. There they fashion little syringes made from reeds and sticks which can be manipulated to squirt water on others as they run along. The people walk up and down the streets, pouring water on all they meet and getting water splashed on them in return.

Two Eastern Legends

One legend that has become a classic in Christmas books dates back to Epiphany night. As the Magi were leaving for their journey eastward, Mary took one of the Babe's swaddling bands and gave it to them as a reward for their gifts. It was received by the kings as a great honor. At the same hour there appeared to them an angel in the form of the star which had been their guide on the way to Bethlehem. It was there to lead them home.

In Lebanon and Syria it is believed, according to legend, that all the rivers and fountains of the world became suddenly holy on Epiphany Eve. All wild beasts were rendered as harmless as doves. Another story is that all trees bowed down in adoration of the Christ child because he was on his way to Jordan to be baptized. That is, every tree except the mulberry and fig knelt down as He passed by. The mulberry was too proud because it provided silk, and the fig tree remained standing erect because the Master had previously cursed it.

3. WINTER FESTIVALS

CHINA, STAR FESTIVAL

When New Year's is over, the Chinese calendar provides that on the eighteenth day of the lunar year men should "thank their lucky stars," and that day is known as the Star Festival. To the Chinese, the planets and constellations are not empty worlds, but the abodes of sainted heroes who not only rule the skies but strongly influence the course of human destinies. Sacrifice is due these spirits; therefore in the night, during the third watch, when all the stars are shining, an altar table is set up in the courtyard, facing north. Upon it are placed two rough prints in colors, one representing the Star Gods, the other the cyclical signs so closely related to them, also a sealed envelope containing a chart of lucky and unlucky stars.

The master of the house first worships the heavenly hosts in a group, then makes a special prayer to the star which presided over his birth. This he does on his personal anniversary, but repeats at the time of the first moon because the New Year in China is supposed to be the birthday of every man.

The food offerings on the star table are insignificant—only three or five bowls of rice balls cooked in sugar and flour. But one

25

hundred and eight little lamps are disposed before the star tablets and lighted by the head of the house. These have special wicks or spills made of red and yellow paper, and the oil in them is perfumed. When they burn out, a matter of only a few minutes, each son of the house comes forward and makes obeisance to his own star by relighting three lamps. According to the brightness of the flame, he knows whether good or bad luck awaits him.

Women were forbidden to take part in this festival, and were supposed to hide until it was over. Then they might join the family group and share in the *t'ang yüan*, or "round sweets," offered on the altar table. In this manner, the family remembered the familiar deities with whom it had been on intimate terms throughout the year.

HAWAII, NARCISSUS FESTIVAL

The Narcissus Festival, an international show of music and dancing that takes place during several weeks in January and February, is one of Hawaii's most spectacular celebrations. The purpose of the festival, which is sponsored by the Chinese Chamber of Commerce, is to promote culture and trade relations with other countries. For tourists, it offers a way to get the "feel" of the Chinese community and become acquainted with its customs, shops, restaurants, and markets. The events that attract most tourists include: a walking tour of Chinatown, a home garden tour, a narcissus and orchid show, and a trade show.

The Narcissus Festival is climaxed by a royal ball given at one of Honolulu's plush hotels. It is preceded by a traditional Lion Dance, which is followed by the procession with the Narcissus Queen and her royal court. Lantern bearers—youthful children of different races dressed in native costumes—put on a pageant projecting an international theme adopted by the Chinese Chamber of Commerce each year, 1970 being the "Year of the Dog."

A queen is chosen to serve as an ambassador of the Chinese community throughout the festival. She is attended at all times by Chinese girls from the University of Hawaii. They are attired in full-length gowns, complemented with beautiful Mandarin jackets. It is their duty to help meet the guests.

As the Queen and her royal court enter the hotel for the Coronation Ball, ten thousand firecrackers are exploded to ward off evil spirits. Fragrance of Narcissus blooms and incense permeate the entrance to the ballroom. Ornate symbols of good luck, happiness, and longevity, designed by Chinese artists, enhance the decor of foyers and stage. The Queen is crowned by the governor of the Islands and a formal dinner takes place.

Tickets for the Narcissus Coronation Ball are in charge of the Chinese sororities of the University of Hawaii, whose scholarship fund will benefit from the proceeds. Following a program of international entertainment, guests dance to the music of a famous orchestra, sometimes until early dawn.

JAPAN

Reading Poems at the Imperial Palace, January 17

The custom of holding an Imperial Poem-reading Ceremony, for the purpose of hearing poems composed for the New Year, is traced back to 1483. A function for this purpose was held on January 17 in the reign of Emperor Gotsuchi—Mikado, 103rd Emperor of Japan. At this classic function a set of about thirty *tanka*, poems of a type containing thirty-one syllables in 5–7–5–7–7 syllabic arrangement, were read. The reading takes places in the Imperial Palace, and their Majesties, the Emperor and Empress and other members of the Imperial family attend.

When all are seated, the officials in charge of the ceremony read the poems before them. The ceremony progresses in a dignified manner as the beautiful poems are read one by one in a deep musical voice and a cadence somewhat similar to that of of the Noh dramatic recital. The few poems by the commoners are read first, in order of their excellence. They are read once, but those composed by princesses may be repeated twice and and ones by the Empress three times. The poem composed by the Emperor is recited last and repeated five times.

Tanka, which means "a short song," consists of five phrases of 5–7–5–7–7 syllables respectively. The poet often suggests a mood or idea and relies upon the reader's imagination and experience to fill in the gap. Thus:

> Clinging to a twig
> Hangs a locust's empty shell;
> With what shining wings
> To far-off heights we know not
> Soars now its soul, I wonder?

CANDLEMAS, FEBRUARY 2

Candlemas is a church festival celebrated on February 2; commemorating, in the Eastern Church, the Presentation of Christ in the Temple; in the Western, the Purification of the Virgin Mary. The Armenian church calls it the Coming of the Son of God into the Temple. The blessing of the altar candles, for which the day is named, is the main feature of the festival.

The day is observed generally wtih candlelight processions. In Europe the custom probably goes back to the ancient torchlight processions for purifying and invigorating fields prior to the sowing season. In Mexico, February 2 corresponds to the Aztec

Year, observed with renewed fires and celebration, especially at the end of the periodic *nemontemi,* the five days of inactivity and sorrowing. The festival retains features of agricultural spring rituals.

GROUNDHOG DAY, FEBRUARY 2

Groundhog Day is a time for forecasting weather for the next six weeks. This custom was brought to America by immigrants from Great Britain and Germany. On February 2, the weather is a most important affair, for on that date the good or bad luck for sowing and planting is determined according to omens. If the groundhog comes out of his hole on February 2 and sees his shadow, he will go back in and stay six more weeks. So if the day is sunny, winter will continue and the result will be bad crops; if it is cloudy, the groundhog will see no shadow, and the reverse will be true. These notions prevail on the Continent and in England, but in Germany it is the badger which breaks the hibernation habit to observe the skies.

29

In Missouri, Groundhog Day was officially established as February 2 by the legislature. In the early part of the present century, a group of merry wags living in and around Quarryville, Lancaster County, Pennsylvania, organized the Slumbering Groundhog Lodge. On the morning of February 2 its members don silk hats and carry canes and go into the fields seeking the burrow of a woodchuck. When one finds a burrow, he calls to the others and all assemble to await the wakening of the animal from his hibernation and his emergence into the outer air. They watch his behavior and then return to the village where they interpret his actions and report them.

VALENTINE'S DAY, FEBRUARY 14

There have been valentines from the beginning of time. Yet, oddly enough, the man who originally offered himself as a valentine had nothing so romantic in mind. St. Valentine was a young Roman who was martyred for refusing to give up Christianity. He died A.D. 270 on February 14, the very day that, by coincidence, had been devoted to love lotteries and to fine-feathered friendships. According to legend, he left a farewell note for a jailer's little daughter, who had befriended him in prison, and signed it "from your Valentine."

It is true that now, almost everywhere, St. Valentine's Day has become, outwardly at least, a much degenerated festival. Beaux still send valentines with colorful printed designs and sentimental verses; candy in red satin boxes; heart-shaped, beautifully packaged perfume; or flowers—but only as a "greeting" and not as a "proposal."

Children like a valentine box, with a slit in the top, in which to mail their valentines at school. There is a town in Colorado named "Loveland" whose post office does a land-office business during this special holiday. The postmaster stamps "Loveland" with an appropriate red seal on the valentines that come to him for this purpose, and drops them in the mail again.

ALASKA, ICEWORM "WINTER WONDERLAND" FESTIVAL

Approximately the first week in February

Back in the Gold Rush days a bored newspaperman invented the Iceworm, an imaginary form of northern life whose chirping in cold winter nights keeps people awake. Cordova, Alaska, perpetuates the hoax the first week in February with an exuberant Iceworm "Winter Wonderland" Festival. For five days visitors from far and near take part in winter sporting events, and an Alaskan beauty earns the honor of being named "Miss Iceworm" of the season. One of the main attractions of the festival is the posters tacked up in various parts of town reading as follows:

> $25.00 Reward!
> For Prompt Return
> Of Iceworm's Tail

It's that time again! Poor Mr. Iceworm has lost his tail. He wants to have it back for the Iceworm Parade. He must have it a half hour prior to the parade time at the very latest.

It seems some culprit went and hid the tail. He'll be leaving

clues around the town for you to find. They'll also be giving clues on Klam. One clue will be given each day.

Mr. Iceworm says he will give a reward of $25.00 to the person who finds his tail. The finder may turn the tail into Palmer McCarter at City Hall.

Clues will be posted in local businesses. The tail is hidden somewhere in city limits. It positively is not hidden on private property.

CARNIVAL

A carnival is a celebration of merrymaking and feasting when people dress in costume, throng the streets, and indulge in all sorts of noisy pranks such as parading, tooting horns, singing, and pelting passers-by with confetti and flowers. Many wear masks and as they go along toss out gifts, which may be small baubles, beads, bangles, whistles, balls, and the like.

In Catholic countries carnivals take place in the last days before Lent and the climax occurs on Shrove Tuesday. In northern communities, when winter comes, athletes from all over the world attend winter carnivals where spectacular sporting events take place. Even though these carnivals are held at extreme distances and in different countries, they have several things in common: floats, torch processions, dances, fireworks, noisemaking, and general tomfoolery. Each elects a king and a queen, and in all there is a spirit of fun throughout the celebration.

United States, Mardi Gras

The most important carnival in the United States takes place in New Orleans, beginning with the Twelfth Night Revels and ending with Mardi Gras on Shrove Tuesday. During the Mardi Gras season some sixty gala balls and countless private parties take place, in addition to the parades. Fifteen or more floats, elaborately designed with a common theme, comprise the substance of each parade. Added to these are innumerable jazz bands and military marching units filling out every procession until it extends for thirty of forty blocks. The most spectacular parades are at night; everyone seems to slip more easily into the carnival spirit after dark.

To a nonresident, Mardi Gras is a blend of four fast-paced days in an old and exotic city. The events are planned by private social organizations called *Krewes*, which produce the parades and finance the balls. Parades are for everyone, but the balls are private affairs, open by invitation only. The Mystic Krewe of Comus, oldest of the city carnival groups, set the pattern in 1857 by staging a lavish parade followed by a ball. The parade and ball pattern has now been adopted by dozens of organizations to celebrate the carnival. Among the oldest and most honorable of the Krewes are the Pacifici, Comos, Carnival German, and Potens. To Rex, largest of the groups, goes the honor of having the carnival's official royalty—the King and Queen of Rex.

CARNIVALS IN EUROPE

France, Carnival at Nice

One of the great celebrations of Europe is the carnival at Nice, where all day and far into the night grotesque, caricatured figures of fact and fiction possess the city. The weird creatures with deformed nodding heads parade down avenue de la Gare, and the streets are alive with many colored lights and large, gorgeous butterflies caught in golden webs hung across the avenue. The king of the carnival, dressed in striped hose and a slashed doublet, grasping in his hands a septre in the image of a jester with cap and bells, leads the parade on a float draped with purple velvet.

Many of the floats are subtly sarcastic, as only the French can be, and people in the streets roar with laughter as they pass by. Many favorite characters are taken out of storage year after year, such as the gigantic cabbages and carrots and gnomes and elfin people that lead the parade. Next come devils mounted on horseback followed by eight horses dragging a papier-mâché lion twenty feet high. On top stands Tartain of Turocon to tame the wild beast. Behind can be seen the Washwoman of Var, followed by every wonder of make-believe extravagance as the nymphs and fairies appear, supplementing the grotesque.

As the fun becomes ever more exciting, the spectators fill the streets and bombard each other with confetti and pellets. Around their necks are worn garlands of flowers, and even the donkeys and carts brought in from the marketplaces receive their share of the decorations.

Belgium, Great Gilles Carnival

The Great Gilles Carnival takes place on Shrove Tuesday, but festivities start six weeks in advance. This undoubtedly has the most famous carnival procession in Belgium and one of the finest and strangest to be seen in Europe. It has it's origin in the "Ballet of the Incas" presented in 1540 by Mary of Hungary, ruler of the Netherlands, in honor of Charles V who had just conquered Peru. So deep are the roots in popular tradition that everyone, from highest to lowest, considers it an honor to be a *gille* ("clown") and to wear the tall headdress of ostrich feathers, the jingling bells and quaint costume, and to dance tirelessly through the streets to a haunting tune. As the gilles dance, they bombard onlookers with thousands of oranges, symbolic of the treasures of Peru. In the evening fireworks burst in a riot of color against the night sky.

Spain and Portugal

In Spain and Portugal, the villagers taking part in the carnival parade decorate their cars with masses of blossoms. When they see their neighbors and friends they throw petals at them, and those standing on the sidelines try to dodge them and pass them back. Some of the towns even hold a battle of flowers. In large cities, there are not only masquerade balls but also bull fights.

Adults and children alike end carnival by throwing flowers and confetti in the streets.

Italy, Parade of the Months

In Italy, *Carnevale* always begins on January 17 and continues until Ash Wednesday. In Cambria and a number of other cities, a Parade of the Months is a carnival event. It includes allegorical figures, representing the twelve months, who pay homage to the "king" who is attended by four harlequins. The months sing traditional verses to the king and later, as the procession moves from place to place, the harlequins are crowned as members of the king's retinue. The ceremony ends with a great banquet for the participants.

Greece, Cheese Week

The general gaiety of carnival, the dancing and masquerading, the licentiousness and exhuberance, reach their highest peak in the last week before Lent, which is called *Cheese Week*. But on the last day, toward sunset, when the bells ring for evensong, the noise quiets down and the faithful slowly make their way toward the church. They are about to enter the long, gray desert-land of fasting and concentration—Lent—and they want to enter it cleansed of all their sins that burden their souls. During the evening service, priests and congregation give each other mutual forgiveness. The parishioners stand in a row, according to age;

the younger members walk over to their elders, kiss their hands and say: "Forgive me," to which the older members reply: "May you be forgiven."

The last dish of Cheese-Sunday dinner is usually eggs. This accounts for the popular saying, "With an egg I close my mouth, with an egg I shall open it again," meaning the red, hard-boiled Easter egg with which the long Lenten fast comes to an end. In Eastern Rumelia the diners roll their eggs across the table, saying, "May Lent roll by even as this egg rolls." Then they stuff their mouths with the egg. In other regions, the last egg left over from the meal is hung from the ceiling by a string; the guests, sitting around the table, hit at the egg with their foreheads to make it swing around, and then try to catch it with their lips.

VIRGIN ISLANDS

Carnival is one of the few festivities in the Virgin Islands in which everyone takes part. The celebration is usually at the end of April and everybody, including the babies, the donkeys, and the dogs, wear fancy carnival hats with tassels and feathers. A little prince and princess dressed in royal costumes proudly march at the head of the children's parade, which consists of floats with fairy-tale themes. The islanders love to dance. The children especially like the calypso, in which they move their feet slowly while their shoulders and hips jut out in all directions. Sometimes boys dance on high stilts that make a scratchy noise.

MEXICO, ST. MARTIN'S CARNIVAL

In the village of Huxquilucan, Mexico, a unique carnival event takes place each year. It is in the form of a battle perpetuating a long existing feud between two churches over their respective saints:

The saint in the church of San Juan is a humble little Virgin de la Candelana, who is dressed in a pink dress and a white veil and crown. Around her neck are several strings of beads and she wears silver earrings with sparkling stones. In one hand is a doll infant and in the other a bouquet of flowers tied with a ribbon.

On the opposite side of town in the church of St. Martin is a

36

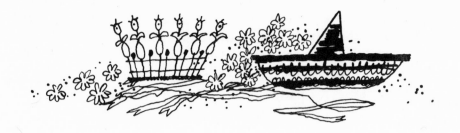

small, elegantly dressed statue of the saint. He is on horseback, wearing a handsomely embroidered sombrero, a bullet belt, silver spurs, and carrying a pistol. The people of the church adore him and array him each year in a new suit and splendid hat.

But the people in St. Martin's Church feel that, even with his fine clothes, their saint must be lonely, so they have invented a little love affair for him. It has become common gossip that every night he rides over to the San Juan Church to visit the Virgin while San Jancito holds his horse outside. The people of San Juan also love their Virgin very much and resent aspersions against her reputation. They indignantly deny that their Virgin would receive a man in the night, even though he were a saint.

On Tuesday of the carnival, the battle of the two churches begins late in the afternoon, with the friends of each side helping and the rest of the inhabitants looking on. The battle is so spirited that the contestants are required to put up barriers of boards about thirty feet high, leaving a short space between them. Both sides use as missiles various kinds of firecrackers, bad eggs, egg shells filled with paint, and in the end, sticks and stones. The conflict goes on for about two hours until authorities force both sides to retire. It is never known which side wins because both claim victory. But there are always some wounded to prove the fight was a good one.

SOUTH AMERICA

Peru, Water-Throwing Carnival

A feature of every carnival in Peru is water-and-flour throwing, and bathing. People throw water and flour from balconies on innocent persons who happen to be passing. Groups of young men enter homes of girl friends and a battle follows in which the boys throw the girls into fountains and bathtubs and vice versa. At carnival dances in the best clubs young men and women spray water on each other from syringes sold for the purpose. There are also water-throwing battles between sailboats on the lake, and in private homes.

Peru, Zafa-casa, or Finishing of the House

Huancayo is a village near Lima where Indian huts are distinguished by tin crosses attached to the roof. The crosses are gaily colored with bright Inca symbols painted on them. The symbols might include an olive branch, flags, guardian angels, a blue-and-white dove, and many species of birds. At the very top of the cross is a little cock to make the family early risers.

When the building of a new house in the village is about to be finished, male relatives and friends cooperate by completing the roof, and women bring food and drinks. This calls for a hilarious fiesta called *Zafa-casa*, or "finishing of the house." Late in the afternoon the villagers arrive and with them are two gaily costumed *nueras*—so-called daughter-in-law and son-in-law, who act as godparents of the festivities. The *nueras* bring small brooms of wild grass and a cross adorned with bright ribbons. Shortly

afterward, the owners of the house appear, looking like beggars, to greet their guests. The man leans heavily on a cane and the woman is shabbily dressed—an indication they had spent their strength and all their money in the building of their house. At the same time, they present their children, who are dressed in new clothes, to show that they have not been made to suffer and that their inheritance will be generous.

When all are in the house, the "decrepit" owners heartily embrace their friends; then the dancing and feasting begin. Early in the evening, the cross and brooms are nailed onto the eaves of the roof as the *nueras* rain flowers over them, so that *Taita Dios* ("Little Father God") may always bless the house.

Peru, Baby's First Haircut

It is the custom among the Indians at Peru and Bolivia to hold a little fiesta to celebrates a baby's first haircut. The hair is left to grow until the baby is a few years old, then relatives and friends are invited to take part in the ceremony. The baby is seated on a high chair like a little king or queen, and the hair is combed and parted into as many locks as there are guests and tied with a bright colored ribbon. The godfather, or mayor of the village, cuts off the first lock and states his gift—which is considerable: sometimes an animal, a piece of land, or a goodly sum of money. The remaining locks are cut off by other guests, each making a gift of money, which pays for the expenses of the *fiesta*, or may be saved for the child. Thus the first stone of his future capital is laid.

Brazil—Carnival in Rio

Carnival in Rio de Janeiro is one of the rarest celebrations the world over. During the four days of carnival (Saturday until Ash Wednesday), thousands of visitors join Brazilians and dedicate themselves to forgetting reality and ignoring tomorrow. A city of almost four hundred thousand inhabitants winds itself up into a nonstop frenzy of parades.

Carnival takes place during Brazil's summer when life revolves around the surf scenes of Rio's famous beaches. Flamengo, Copacabana, Leblon, and Fora are among the most popular bathing places in the world. Unlike many seaside resorts in other countries, Rio's strands know no social snobbery, rich and poor bask side by side.

In the streets are hundreds of rambling food and drink vendors, teams of soccer and volleyball players, and small boys who stage aerial kite fights, applying a mixture of ground glass to the string to cut their opponent's line.

In the last week before Carnival, the atmosphere in any of Rio's many samba schools is one of barely controlled hysteria. At Mangueira, for example, which is located on the edge of one of the mountainside slums mythologized in the movie *Black Orpheus*, the night air is filled with the screech of whistles, the relentless pounding of drums, and the contortions of thousands of dancers, who for one hour will march in the main parade that marks the sensational climax to nearly a year of preparation.

There are *three* principal aspects to Rio's Carnival that might be called organized. There are the costume balls, the street carnival (the parade of samba schools along Avenida Presidente Vargas), and the *blocos*, which are street parades held by the inhabitants of the individual city blocks. But the action starts long before this. Night clubs and discotheques throw parties for all comers; there are spontaneous parades that consist of anything from a couple of dozen costumed revelers to a string of elaborate floats.

By far the most famous features of Carnival are the balls. Of the dozen that take place, most are given by semiprivate organizations such as athletic and social clubs. The balls that count are the Yacht Club (the Friday night before Carnival), the Copacabana, Artists' and Writers', and poshest of all, the Municipal Ball on the final night. Tickets for this grand event cost fifty dollars and up.

The single event of Carnival that should not be missed under any circumstance is the parade of the samba schools on the final night. It is unquestionably one of the most dramatic sights and sounds in the world. The parade route—lined with judges, spectators, press, police, T.V. and movie crews—is along Avenida Presidente Vargas. Gigantic illuminated decorations are suspended over the streets.

The lead dancers, bearing their school's banner, swoop to the head of the formations; the others fall in behind them and the parade begins. The wide avenue is filled with its extravagant dance routines and dandified costumes, usually a blend of eighteenth century wigs for the men and great tiers of crinoline for the women. Costumes often cost well over a thousand dollars apiece.

It may take an hour or more for one school of brightly costumed dancers to pass the judges stand. Individual dancers upstage one another with routines that combine juggling with gymnastics and a free form of choreography that defies description. Every school also has a song specially composed for each Carnival; it is chanted

41

over and over by the paraders as they follow the route. Some schools have a king, a bewigged, bearded figure in resplendent robes with a train carried by ten or more men.

Hours later, when the best part of the parade is over, the rest will be taken up with processions of floats and bands, and spectators will drift away to where the third organized feature of Carnival—the *bloco*—is taking shape. Bloco is Portuguese for block, and the general idea is that any city-block dwellers who feel like it can organize their own parade, sometimes with floats and pretty girls in costume, but always with dancing and music. A band and some musicians will start beating a samba and anyone so inclined joins in and follows the music. The *bloco* may last for hours, winding up in someone's swimming pool or exhausting itself on one of the many beaches.

People who have never seen Rio's Carnival tend to think of it as a commercial event designed to attract the tourist trade. It is nothing like that. The spirit is one of elation and the mood of the celebrants is one of simplicity and joy.

PURIM, HEBREW FEAST

Purim, a Jewish semifestival, is celebrated in February. It commemorates the joyousness of the Jews when Queen Esther interceded with King Ahasuerus for deliverance of her people from Haman's vengeance. "Purim" means "lots" because the day for the extermination of the Persian Jews was determined by casting lots. The day before is known as the Feast of Esther and the following day is observed as Purim.

In many ways Purim has the spirit of a carnival; there are parties, masquerades, costume plays, and dances. The fun of Purim begins with the stamping of children's feet and the noise of *greggers* ("wooden rattles") whenever, on the evening and morning of Purim, Haman's name is used during the reading of the Book of Esther in the synagogue. Then there are child actors who go from house to house in Jewish communities in Europe acting out the story of Esther in humorous form, singing comic Purim songs, and collecting money for charity. Giving "alms to the poor," to children in children's homes, to older folks in homes for the aged, to patients in hospitals, and exchanging gifts with friends and relatives add a note of consideration of others to their sheer enjoyment of Purim.

SHROVE TUESDAY

In the old days Lent often meant wearing dark, drab clothing, eating meals without meat, and banning all good times for the

forty days. And so it became the custom for people to have a time of jolly fun on Shrove Tuesday, the day before Lent began. It was a time of gay celebration, of carnival and revelry, of costume parades and merrymaking, of tricks and fun poking.

In Europe Shrove Tuesday is still called "Pancake Day" in many countries. On this day the special menu in most homes is pancakes and sausages, bacon, or scraps of meat served with other good things to eat (and so the day is called Guddin's Day in some places!). Frying pancakes for her family gives the housewife the opportunity to use up left-over lard and meat scraps before the fast of Lent begins.

4. LENT

The word Lent is of Anglo-Saxon origin, meaning spring, but to Christians it is a forty-day period of self-examination and repentance in preparation for the Easter festival. There are several reasons for the forty-day season—to commemorate the forty days Moses spent on Mount Sinai, the forty years wandering, the forty days Jesus spent in the desert, or the forty hours in the tomb. To most people it is a period of strengthening their faith in the Lord, through the media of repentance and prayer.

To most Christians, Lent is a period of quietness and meditation symbolizing the ancient words of Jesus to the tired activist: Come ye into the desert and rest a while. For people burdened by many responsibilites and sometimes confused decisions, a few weeks of quiet contemplation help to renew strength and deepen insights into world problems. For almost a thousand years the Catholic Church followed a norm laid down by Pope Saint Gregory the Great for fasting during the Lenten season: "We abstain from flesh meat and from all things that come from the flesh as milk, cheese, eggs and butter." According to a new ruling of the Ecumenical Council in Rome, Roman Catholics are obligated to fast only on two days during Lent: Ash Wednesday and Good Friday.

The fasting rules appointed by the Greek Orthodox Church are still very strict, especially for "Great Lent," the six weeks before Easter as opposed to "Little Lent," the twenty-five days preceding Christmas. It is forbidden to eat any animal product: meat, eggs, fish, milk products; on Wednesdays and Fridays, and during the whole week preceding Easter (Holy Week), even wine and olive oil are ruled out. It is usually the womenfolk who keep this absolute fast; they are generally honored by other villagers, who show their respect by setting a table for them with special dishes: walnut cakes, bean soup, must-syrup, and by bringing them useful gifts.

Ancient Lenten Calendars

It is natural that Lent should seem very slow in passing for those who fast. For this reason, in the days when there were no calendars to tell people how near they were to getting to the end of the fasting period, several ingenious time-reading systems were contrived. For instance, the figure of a nun—representing Lent—was cut out in paper; she was drawn as a woman without a mouth (abstention from food), with her hands crossed in prayer. She had seven feet (the seven weeks of fasting.) This paper figure was hung on the wall, and every Saturday the fasters tore off one of her seven feet. In certain provinces in Greece a different method was used: seven feathers from a hen were stuck in a

46

boiled potato or an onion hanging from the ceiling by a string. There it remained throughout Lent; the feathers were removed in turn as each week went by. It was called *Kukaras* and was an object of great fear to the children of the house; parents used it as a threat to make them behave.

ASH WEDNESDAY

Ash Wednesday marks the beginning of Lent for Catholics of the Latin rite as well as for some Protestant churches. On this day priests will repeat the admonishment, "Remember, man, that thou art dust and unto dust thou shalt return," as they place the mark of the cross of ashes on the foreheads of the faithful.

The ashes are made from the branches of brushwood or palms which were consecrated the previous year on Palm Sunday. They are sifted, cleaned, and given a special blessing before they are distributed on Ash Wednesday. The custom of strewing ashes on the head in form of a cross is a sign of humility and penitence.

WORLD DAY OF PRAYER

A day when the whole world prays is a modern Lenten custom with age-old roots. All around the world, on the first Friday of Lent, there are groups of Christians earnestly praying that Christ's will be done and that his peace may come to all the earth. Even the children and youth in many places have special prayer services and programs.

Seventy-five years ago, a few scattered women's missionary bands in the United States set aside the Day of Prayer. Now in more than a hundred and forty nations around the world, hundreds of thousands of Christians keep up a continuous chain of prayer throughout the day. The World Day of Prayer is sponsored by the World Council of Churches and the offerings brought by the worshippers are used to help answer prayers for peace and good will.

MOTHERING SUNDAY (FOURTH SUNDAY IN LENT)

This charming custom originated in England where, on the last Sunday in Lent, boys and girls who lived away from home

were allowed to go back to the Mother Church in which they had been baptized or brought up. They carried with them gifts to place in front of the altar. The Mother prefix means "home or refuge," thus the origin of the term "Mother Church," "Mother's Day," the old saying: "He who goes a-mothering finds violets in the lane."

The Sunday is also celebrated according to the popular meaning of the word, much as Mother's Day is celebrated in America. Young people who live away from home return on that day to visit their mothers. Those in domestic service are given a holiday and the returning boys and girls do the chores.

LAETARE SUNDAY

The fourth Sunday in Lent is also called Laetare Sunday. As a symbol of joy for the day (Mid-Lent), the Pope used to carry a golden rose in his hand while celebrating Mass. Originally it was a single rose of natural size, but since the fifteenth century it has consisted of a cluster or branch of roses made of pure gold and set with precious stones. The Pope blesses it every year and often confers it upon churches, shrines, or dignitaries as a token of esteem. In case of such a bestowal, a new rose is made during the subsequent year.

An adaptation of this Papal custom is Notre Dame's annual award (since 1888): a medal to an American lay Catholic who has distinguished himself in science, literature, philosophy, or sociology. The medal is made of heavy gold with black enamel tracings of a rose.

Palm Sunday has been thus named to commemorate Christ's triumphant arrival in Jerusalem, when people of the holy city strewed his path with palm branches in sign of reverence. From very early days Christian churches have ordered that branches be carried in procession on that day.

In Protestant churches palms are often distributed to the congregation and a special sermon and music are prepared for the occasion. In Catholic churches a service called "Blessing of the Palms," which includes a number of superb prayers relating to the imagery of the palms, is observed. During the morning Mass, a history of the Passion according to St. Matthew is sung by three clerics vested in white albs and black stoles. The chant is a solemn and beautiful melody in different pitches. One (tenor) represents the evangelist; the second(high tenor) chants the voices of different people and crowds; and the third (bass) sings only the words of Christ.

In Czechoslovakia, where Palm Sunday is known as *Kvetna Nedele,* the priests bless pussy willows. Following the Sunday service, the farmers wave the willows over their fields of grain, hoping they will not have hail or violent windstorms. Finnish children also search for pussy willows in the woods. If the winter has been severe the buds will not be out, and they cut off birch branches, which they decorate with paper flowers and bright feathers for Easter Day.

In Mexico, *Domingo de Palmas* is the occasion for a walking garden. Children and their families carry large bouquets of frag-

49

rant flowers, palms, and laurel to the church to receive the blessing by the priest. The Mexicans carefully keep the flowers until next year for protection from sickness.

In Greece, wherever palm trees grow, the churches are decorated outside and inside with palm leaves; in the provinces farther north, bay and myrtle are used instead. On Palm Sunday, palm leaves are ingeniously woven into various shapes, such as small baskets, half-moons, stars, and above all, crosses. After the service, the priest stands at the church door and hands each parishioner a branch of bay or myrtle and a small palm-woven cross. This memento is called *vaya,* and it is afterwards stuck in the frame of one of the family icons. Protective and curative powers are generally ascribed to it.

PALM SUNDAY IN ROME

The greatest of Palm Sunday processions is held in Rome, where the holiday is called *Domenica Delle Palme.* The Pope, seated in St. Peter's chair, carried on the shoulders of eight men, appears and blesses the palms. The branches are carefully saved and burned to make next year's Ash Wednesday's ashes.

The scene of the blessing of the palms in St. Peter's Square is dazzling. The cardinal celebrating mass moves about the altar in a purple robe with a long train, surrounded by assistants in vestments richly embroidered in gold. At one side are seated the canons in rich crimson silk and little white ermine capes, and opposite them the monsignori in black, trimmed with fine white lace, and gray squirrel capes. After the service, the blessed golden palms are distributed among the clergy, the olive branches to the congregation. Then the cardinal, canons, and monsignori and all the rest go in procession onto the square, emerging from one door and re-entering through another, thus symbolizing the entry of Christ into Jerusalem.

5. HOLY WEEK

Holy Week is a week of general mourning throughout the Christian world. It celebrates the last days in the life of Christ and recapitulates those events that have particular significance in shaping the Christian religion. The week actually begins on the eve of Palm Sunday and ends at midnight before Easter. There was a time when all the days of the week were to be free from weekly occupation and devoted to religious exercises. But later, the church decided to hold the services in the evening, instead of in the morning, for the benefit of working people, and to retain only Good Friday as a holiday. The Roman Catholic Church has a complete Missal, "The Sacred Tridumm of Holy Week," for services on Holy Thursday, Good Friday, and Easter Vigil. Sometimes special services are held each noon hour, and a visiting pastor of prominence is engaged to give the meditation.

GREEK ORTHODOX HOLY WEEK

In Greek Orthodox churches, the church bells remain silent throughout Holy Week; in the language of the people the bells are "widowed," and the faithful are called to mass by the town criers. It is a week of sacred devotion, and singing, music, plays, and entertainment in any form are forbidden. The last holy days are celebrated much as in other Christian churches, but the first three have a definite theme of their own.

Monday. Only one kind of activity is permitted; house cleaning, sweeping, and in general preparing for Easter. We are reminded that Jewish women are also doing a special job of house cleaning at this time of year. All leaven and leavened bread must be disposed of before time for Passover.

Tuesday. On the evening of Tuesday in Holy Week the service is devoted chiefly to reading a passage in the Gospel referring to Mary Magdalene, who poured myrrh over the feet of Christ. Most of the hymns sung during this service likewise refer to Mary Magdalene.

Wednesday is devoted generally to the anointment of the faithful. This anointment takes place after the morning service. Those who are unable to go to church because of sickness or age are anointed at home by their relatives. It is also the custom to enclose in an envelope a small wad of cotton wool dipped in holy oil and mail it to fathers, husbands, and sons who are at sea or settled in distant countries where there are no orthodox churches.

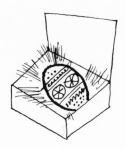

Maundy Thursday. In Greek Orthodox churches, Easter preparation usually begins on the morning of Maundy Thursday. That is when the Easter eggs are dyed; the traditional color is red, and for this reason Maundy Thursday is often called Red Thursday. In some of the villages it is the custom to draw various designs on the eggs, either before dyeing them, with melted wax, or after they have been dyed, with a needle. In the evening the eggs are placed in a small box and taken to the church to be blessed.

In all Christian churches, Holy Thursday commemorates our Lord's Last Supper with His disciples. It was on a Thursday evening that Jesus celebrated the Passover in the upper room of a Jewish friend's home. The Catholic Mass of Holy Thursday is one of the most solemn of the year. The priests are dressed in white vestments, the liturgical color of joy, and the cross is covered with a white veil. All the bells in the church are rung and continue to ring until the Gloria is finished. From that moment the bells have a wooden clapper and are not heard again until the Gloria on Sunday morning. In many European countries the silence of the bells is explained to the children by the popular expression "the bells have gone to Rome."

GOOD FRIDAY

On Good Friday the Passion of our Lord is commemorated as related in the Gospel of St. John (John 18:1-40). In Catholic churches the altars are completely unadorned, without cross, without linen, without veils. All the statuary is covered with mourning cloth.

Tre Ore Service. Tre Ore ("Three Hours") is a well-known Good Friday service of devotion beginning at noon and continuing until three in the afternoon. It was first performed in Lima, Peru, by Father Alphonso Messia and quickly spread to other parts of the world. In America the service is commonly used by both Protestant and Catholic churches. The three-hour devotion is usually built around the last Seven Words of the Cross. At other times the three-hour period is divided into units of one hour each, each one of which is used to present a complete service of worship in the development of some theme.

Stations of the Cross. The devotion known as the Way of the Cross, or stations of the cross, first came into use in Western Christendom in the fifteenth century when pilgrims of the Holy Land marked off sites associated with our Lord's Passion in Jerusalem and its environs, Catholic churches have on their walls pictures or carvings of each scene, fourteen in all. On Good Friday groups of worshippers, united in common prayer, stop at each station and sing hymns (usually the *Stabat Mater*) as they pass from one station to another.

Beginning at midnight on Good Friday in Verne, Furnes, (Belgium) a pilgrims' procession has stopped before the eighteen Stations of the Cross built in 1680. The distance between the different stations is said to correspond to the number of steps taken by Christ from Jerusalem to Mount Calvary—a total of 5,751.

GOOD FRIDAY IN SPAIN

Holy Week in Spain is possibly the outstanding religious celebration, not only in Spain, but in the world. People who view television or have seen Cinerama are familiar with the processions of various religious brotherhoods, each belonging to a church and each representing a scene from the Passion. The procession is made up of huge *pasos,* or floats, carried on the backs of twenty-five or thirty bearers.

The *pasos,* lighted by hundreds of candles and surrounded by flowers, are carried very slowly through the streets, followed by brotherhood members who are dressed in long, pointed black or white hoods who walk barefoot. Some of the *pasos* are beautifully made by famous artists of the past, and nearly all bring home the idea of intense human suffering. The streets are blacked out, and the only sounds are the occasional tolling of the church bells for the dead, and the beat of a single drum which sets the slow pace for the hooded figures, moving stiffly in unison. Frequent halts have to be made to allow bearers of the heavy *pasos* to rest. It is during one or another of these halts that the *Saetas,* songs and impromptu laments, rend the air.

In *Seville* the processions were originally started in the Middle Ages by a number of confraternities. There are now no less than forty-four *pasos*, and each has a chapel in which their paraphernalia is kept between festivals. Many are works of art, elaborately and artistically carved. They are attired for the procession in costly robes, while the details of platforms or stages on which they are carried are in many cases of real silver; some of the cloaks used are embroidered in gold and cost many thousands of dollars. Among the finest *pasos* present on Good Friday are those of the Agony in the Garden, Christ Bearing the Cross, the Crucifixion, and Descent from the Cross.

A wonderful Good Friday procession is also held in Murcia. The wooden images used are the work of a famous sculptor and a trade guild is in charge of each *pasos*. The tailors bear the gigantic group of the Last Supper; the gardeners, that of the Agony in the Garden; the bakers take up the *pasos* of the Kiss of Judas; the shoemakers, the group of St. John, and so forth. All the bearers are dressed in veils and carry candles and musical instruments. A standard bearer comes first, accompanied by a group of boys whose duty it is to proclaim to the crowd: "This is done in rememberance of the Passion of Our Lord Jesus Christ."

The sculptor, Salzillo, is said to have created the group of the Agony in the Garden from a drawing furnished by an angel, whom he had received as a poor man for a night's lodging.

P.70   HOLY SATURDAY

Saturday of Holy Week is a strange interlude in the Easter festival. It commemorates the day Christ rested in the tomb, the only day of his ministry that he was not alive and present with his friends. The mood is quiet in all towns and cities in somber expectancy, which will turn into radiant joy at the first sight of the evening stars. The faithful keep lights burning all night so their rays will link with the morning sun.

Catholic churches hold a Saturday night service leading directly into Easter morning. Vespers begin with two dramatic rituals: blessing the Eastern fires and the paschal candle. The Solemn Mass of Easter begins with the chanting of the Kyrie:

Lord, have mercy on us. Lord, have mercy on us. Lord, have mercy on us.

Christ, have mercy on us,Christ, have mercy on us. Christ, have mercy on us.

Lord, have mercy on us. Lord, have mercy on us. Lord, have mercy on us.

When the choir completes the Kyrie, the priest solemnly intones the Gloria, the bells begin to ring, and the images are unveiled. Then comes the dramatic moment when the celebrant begins the Alleluia. He sings it three times, raising his voice a little each time. All repeat it in the tone the celebrant used.

GREEK ORTHODOX EASTER

In Greek Orthodox churches, it has become customary to hold the Easter Sunday service on Saturday night and to proclaim the Resurrection of the Lord at midnight precisely.

The ceremony of the Resurrection is always held in the open air, usually in the courtyard of the church. Suddenly the door of the sanctuary swings open, and the priest appears holding a lighted candle: "Come ye, partake of the never-setting light and glorify Christ who is risen from the dead," he chants. The congregation crowds around to light their candles from that of the priests. They pass their lights on to their neighbors, until the whole church is ablaze. After the whole congregation has partaken of the light, the priest, followed by banners, cantors, and congregation, leaves the church and steps onto a rough scaffolding erected for the purpose outside. There he reads the Gospel passage describing the Resurrection. Finally he triumphantly intones the psalm: *Christos anesti,* "Christ is risen." The churchbells ring out joyfully, guns and fireworks are set off, and ships at anchor sound their whistles. The faithful turn to each other and say: "Christ is risen!" after which they exchange the kiss of the Resurrection.

PROTESTANT CHURCHES

Protestant churches conduct Easter Vespers, but with no special rituals. A good many Episcopal churches schedule the first Vespers of Easter and the lighting of the paschal candle as an afternoon service for Holy Saturday. Most impressive, perhaps, is the custom of going to a hilltop to watch for Easter dawn. In America and many European countries, multitudes gather in the darkness, and amid a hush of meditation and expectation turn their eyes toward the eastern sky. When accompanied by such notes as those of Handel's immortal air, "I Know That My Redeemer Liveth," the spell is complete.

6. EASTER

In Christian lands the greatest religious festival of the year is Easter. It takes place on the first Sunday following the full moon that appears on or after the vernal equinox, about March 21. It is a joyous day commemorating Christ's Resurrection and Ascension into heaven. The churches are filled with people dressed in new Easter costumes; the altars are banked with lilies and spring flowers; and the choir and congregation join in singing joyous hymns and anthems.

Easter is also a springtime festival; many of its customs and legends are pagan in origin and have nothing to do with Christianity. Like all spring festivals of ancient origin, the celebration is closely tied to nature worship; for instance, the symbolic use of eggs and the Easter hare both have a mystical background. The thread of Easter not only knits the past with the present but sets aside a time for people to take new inspiration because the cold bleak earth grows warm and fair. Every land beholds the miracle and sees in it a promise that life is somehow infinite and eternal.

Many Easter customs have existed since time immemorial, and continue today dressed in new meaning.

SUNRISE SERVICES

It was a common belief among the early Christians that on Easter morning the sun danced in honor of the Resurrection and people rose long before the sun to see the feat. Perhaps this ancient belief is the inspiration for the many sunrise services that take place on Easter morning in all parts of the United States and Europe. A most elaborate sunrise service is staged in the Hollywood Bowl, Hollywood, California, on Easter morning. It was inaugurated in 1921, and every year an estimated crowd of thirty thousand begins to stream in at midnight on Easter Eve to spend the night in a dimly lighted stadium. In front of the band shell are fifty thousand calla lilies, and shortly after dawn a living cross of 250 teen-agers is formed. On the stage is a choir of a hundred adults and a symphony orchestra, and as the sun rises over the mountain the service begins. The choir, accompanied by the orchestra, sings the beautiful *Hallelujah* chorus and other Easter anthems.

THE EASTER PARADE

The custom of taking an Easter walk through fields and country still continues in parts of Europe, but in the United States there is a parade. The traditional Easter parade goes back thousands of years when Constantine commanded his council to bedeck themselves in the more elegant robes to observe the day to honor

Christ's Resurrection. Coupled with this was a popular belief that one must wear for the first time on Easter Sunday a new article of clothing, to ensure good fortune for the rest of the year.

THE EASTER RABBIT

Why the Easter rabbit hippety-hops into the Easter picture has many mystical explanations. In the Orient, the Easter hare is very closely associated with the new moon, and Japanese artists paint its figure across the moon's disc. The Chinese represent the moon as a rabbit pounding rice in a mortar. The Europeans also have all sorts of fantasies connected with the moon, but the most accepted theory is that it represents fertility. However, children like to believe that on Easter Sunday a rabbit, after a long winter's sleep, lays bright red and blue, yellow and purple eggs in the new grass.

In Germany, it is the Easter hare that brings the eggs and hides them in the house and garden for children to search for. In many places pretty little rabbit gardens are made ready for the hare. Children have fun making them of moss or grass to provide a place for the rabbit to hide the eggs. Well known are the eggs made of sugar with little scenes inside that can be seen through a transparent window at one end.

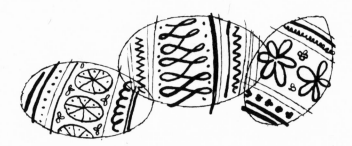

EASTER EGGS

The custom of using eggs in various ways has been associated with Easter for centuries. In Europe, particularly in the Slavic countries, eggs are hand-painted in distinctive traditional designs that are passed down from generation to generation in towns and

60

villages. The giving of Easter eggs as presents was at one time almost universal. After they were colored, various designs and inscriptions were etched into the surface and exchanged by those sentimentally inclined, much as valentines.

Eggs play an important part in Easter sports. Centuries ago, Romans celebrated the Easter season by running races on an oval track and giving eggs as prizes. Most traditional Easter games have the same basic rules, with slight variations, in all Christian countries. Egg rolling by very small children is a universal custom; the origin is said to be symbolic of the rolling away of the stone from Christ's sepulcher.

EASTER FOODS

The tradition of the paschal lamb perhaps inspired the use of the meat of lamb as a popular food at Eastertime. Frequently, however, little figures of a lamb made of butter, pastry, or sugar have been substituted for meat, forming Easter table decorations. Spiced meat of some kind is a popular Easter dish; and of course there is the custom of eating as many eggs as possible for breakfast.

Hot Cross Buns. Many Easter customs have existed from time immemorial and continue today, dressed in a new meaning. The hot cross bun, for example, is pagan in origin. The Anglo-Saxon savages consumed cakes as a part of the jollity that attended the welcoming of spring. The early missionaries from Rome blessed the cakes by drawing a cross upon them. Comes Ash Wednesday hot cross buns appear in every bakery window in the United States and Europe, and interestingly enough, are sold only during the Easter season.

Pretzels. Christians in the Roman Empire made a special dough consisting of flour, salt, and water only, since fat, eggs, and milk were forbidden. They shaped it into the form of two arms crossed in prayer to remind them that Lent was a season of penance and devotion. They called these breads *bracalle* ("little arms"). From the Latin word, the Germans later coined the term *brezel*, or pretzel. In many parts of Europe pretzels are still a Lenten food.

They make their annual appearance on Ash Wednesday, and special vendors sell them on the streets of villages and towns; then they disappear until the next Ash Wednesday.

It is possible that Easter with its extremely dramatic background appeals more strongly to the African than does Christmas. The birth of a child to them is a commonplace occurrence, but suffering, on the other hand, speaks eloquently to every man. Consequently Christ's suffering and death occupie the central part in African Easter. The whole week becomes a silent one from the triumphant entry on Palm Sunday to the final agony on Good Friday.

In Rhodesia there is a preaching service on Friday morning; Saturday is visiting day, but on Easter Sunday a bell is rung at three o'clock in the morning, and all the people go to a hill for a sunrise service. They march singing and have special music for groups and soloists. The minister closes the service with an Easter meditation. Later on during the day young people present a dramatization of the Easter events.

In Matendeudze, near Mutanibra, on Easter, six groups start out before dawn going in different directions to sing the great Easter news, "Christ is risen." As they sing, they accompany themselves with *hoshos* (an African musical instrument resembling a rattle). After visiting homes and villages for twelve hours, the groups meet in a central place to form a large group where all take part in a special Easter service.

LAPP LADY DAY

In Finnish Lapland villages such as Irari and Enontekiö, the Lapps hold a church festival on Lady Day (March 25) which usually coincides with the Easter season. On this occasion, Lapps in their brilliant costumes come from remote homesteads to take part in a special church service, usually followed by a program of festivities, which include lasso-throwing contests and skijoring races with reindeer on the frozen lake. Colorful Lapp weddings are often arranged to take place during these festivities.

7. EARLY SPRING FESTIVALS

Passover and Easter are observed within a few days of each other. Passover commemorates the deliverance of the six hundred thousand Isrealite slaves and their families from Egypt, the land of the Pharaohs. Also it is an agricultural festival associated with the first harvest of the year, the barley harvest. At this time, Jewish farmers journeyed to the temple in Jerusalem with an omer (measure) of grain for a thank offering.

Passover is essentially a family affair. During the days preceding the festival, the house is especially cleaned, the Pesach (Passover) dishes are made ready and the ordinary ones put away, relatives and friends are invited who cannot have a Seder in their own homes. All leaven and leavened bread must be disposed of, for only matzoth, unleavened breads, are eaten during Passover —a reminder of the hurried departure from Egypt with no time for bread to rise.

A special service called the Seder (meaning order of the service) is conducted at home on the first two evenings of Passover by conservative and orthodox Jews, and on the first evening by reform Jews. The form of the service, the story of the Exodus, and folk songs are found in Haggadah (narrative) "a book," which is the focal point of the Seder. In the center of the table is the Seder plate. On it are placed the Passover symbols; a roasted lamb bone and a roasted egg in memory of God's command to Moses on the eve of departure from Egypt and in memory of the festival offerings in the Temple; Maror (a bitter herb), symbolizing the bitter hardships of slavery; parsley and salt water for the bitter tears shed by slaves; Haroset, made of apples, nuts, wine, sugar, and cinnamon, representing the bricks made by the Israelites in Egypt. Matzoth and cups of wine complete the symbols used at the Seder. An extra cup of wine is placed on the table for the eagerly awaited though invisible guest, Elijah, the prophet of hope and faith. During the service the youngest child asks the Four Questions:

"Why is this night different from all other nights? On all other nights we may eat either leavened bread or unleavened. Why, on this night, do we eat only unleavened?"

"On all other nights we may eat all kinds of herbs. Why, on this night, do we eat only bitter herbs?"

"On all other nights, we need not dip an herb even once. Why on this night must we do so twice?"

"On all other nights, we may sit at table erect or leaning. Why on this night, do we sit reclining?"

The narrative of Haggadah is the reply to these questions.

The custom of *Ma'ot Hitim* ("wheat money") is a fund donated for the purchase of matzoth and other Passover products for the poor and needy.

The synagogue service on the first day of Passover includes the prayer for dew in which Jews join their "brethren in Palestine by praying for sufficient dew to overcome the lack of rain during the [Palestinian] summer." On the last day of Passover, a memorial service is held for departed kinfolk.

WHITSUNTIDE

The date of Whitsuntide is always dependent on the date of Easter, for it comes seven weeks and a day after the Festival of the Resurrection. Pentecost occurs the Sunday before to commemorate the day that the Apostles were gathered in the upper room in Jerusalem to celebrate the Jewish festival, Feast of Weeks. Above them appeared tongues as if of fire, which settled upon each of them, and they were all filled with the Holy Spirit and began to speak in foreign tongues. This enabled them to go and evangelize the world.

Whitsuntide is an occasion to express the feelings generated by the return of good weather, the new green of the fields, the spring flowers, and the resurgence of spiritual powers. Each European country seems to have chosen this day or period in the spring season for festivities which include processions, mimes, dances, and general merriment. Perhaps most characteristic of Whitsuntide is the custom of going out into the woods or fields and bringing back green boughs to dress up some member of the village. Thus Green George, Jack-in-the-Green, the Leaf Man, the Whitsuntide Lout are associated with this period in parts of Russia, Switzerland, and the Balkan States.

Procession of Giants. On Whitmonday, the traditional Procession of Giants of Belgium and France takes place in Lille, in the course of which more than a hundred of these fabulous creatures, from twelve to eighteen feet high, are taken in procession through the principal streets of the town. These traditional giants are relics of the Spanish domination of the Netherlands and used to be of wickerwork supported by a light wooden frame. Nowadays, they are often made of plastic materials. Towns that send their Giants to Lille include Bailleul, Cambrai, Valenciennes, Hazebrouck, Denain, and Dunkirk.

In the Black Forest in Germany shepherds buy new bells for their sheep on Whitsuntide. They try them out before they buy them, as each man wants to be sure that all the bells for his flock sound well together, and all day their sounds echo through the woods.

Merchant's Flower Market. In Haarlem, a city in the Netherlands, an unusual celebration takes place at night on Whitsuntide. Merchants arrive in the big market place in the afternoon or early evening. They arrange their flowers on tables and carts—red and

white tulips, yellow daffodils, blue irises, red geraniums. When all the flowers have been arranged, the lights are turned off.

Soon the dark square fills with people. At midnight, the church bells ring out, and at the same time, floodlights go on. As if by magic, the thousands of flowers appear! The festival continues until dawn. Hand organs play and the young people dance. Food stands are set up and people stroll about with armfuls of flowers they have bought for Whitsuntide.

Lazybones. A most unusual custom is the celebration of "Lazybones," the dying winter devil who must be driven out or conquered by ridicule on Whitsuntide. Youngsters in Belgium and Holland especially delight in wakening late sleepers on this occasion, and "Lazybone" may well find old rubbish fastened to his door.

Kneeling Sunday. Whitsunday is commonly known as "Kneeling" Sunday in Greece, because on this day the priest makes three invocations during which the whole congregation and the priest himself remain in a kneeling position. One of these invocations is a prayer for the repose of the dead. The parishioners bring to the church bunches of flowers picked from their gardens; they place these flowers on the ground in front of them as they kneel and burn a candle to light the way for the departing souls. The faithful bow their heads very low and cover their eyes with leaves of rose petals, for, if their eyes remain open when the souls of their dead relatives pass by, there will be recognition and tears and sorrow at this new separation, and the soul will refuse to leave with the others.

Smoke Money. In England, Whitsunday was the day people paid their money for the support of the church. They were assessed according to the number of fireplaces in their houses, or sometimes according to the number of chimneys. So the Whitsunday collection came to be known as "hearth money" or "smoke money."

CORPUS CHRISTI

In the thirteenth century, in a convent near Liége, a young nun, called Juliana of Retinnes (Retinnes being the town of her birth), had a vision of the moon in splendor but with part of the sphere broken away. She implored God's help to understand its meaning, and it was revealed to her that the moon represented the church, but the break indicated the lack of a solemnity in honor of the Eucharist. Three years later, the Pope directed that a celebration in the form of a festival take place in honor of the Blessed Sacrament to be held the eighth Thursday after Easter.

Very early the custom developed of carrying the Holy Sacrament in a splendid procession through the town after Mass on Corpus Christi Sunday. In Catholic countries the procession developed into a splendid pageant of grandeur and devotion. It was led by clerics dressed in white-and-gold vestments, followed by sovereigns and princes, presidents and members of state, magis-

67

trates, members of trade guilds, honor guards of the armed forces, all carrying their own banners, which created a splendid spectacle indeed.

In America the grandeur of the procession is dispensed with except in villages along the Mexican border, but the liturgy is the same everywhere. At the end of the Mass, the celebrant is vested in a cope, and a veil is put around his shoulders; with the ends of this he grasps a gold-and-silver vessel for holding the circular crystal in which the Blessed Sacrament is exposed and faces the people. A procession is formed behind the white standard of the Eucharist, and as the people fall in line, they sing hymns from the office of the day. Whether the procession takes place outside or within the church, everyone returns to the main altar for the benediction.

CORPUS CHRISTI IN EUROPE

It is only in Europe—in Spain, Italy, France, and Portugal— that the grandeur of the procession is still carried on. In many villages the Sacrament is carried over a thick bed of rose petals, and the houses are gaily decorated. Crucifixes and pictures of Christ are prominently displayed from window ledges, steps of cottages, and fountains. In many places people display bright hangings and spread carpets before their houses in honor of the Sacrament.

In Spain, Corpus Christi is a time of pomp and pageantry. The cities known for splendor and color of the festival are Barcelona, Burgos, Cadiz, Toledo, and Seville. In Toledo and Seville, the *pasos* are accompanied by the *Sieses*, six youngsters dressed in medieval ceremonial robes, who have the age-old privilege of spreading flower petals before the sacred Host during the procession. Cathedral walls are covered with priceless tapestries and garlands of flowers. In practically all communities the Corpus Christi festival concludes with a program of regional folk dancing, bullfights, and firework displays.

In Italy. While Corpus Christi processions are held all over the world, the village of Genzano, Italy, has a distinctive feature—the famous *Infiorata.*

The name might be thought to signify the throwing of flowers *over* a religious procession; but on the contrary, it means the adornment of the street through which the procession is to pass with an elaborate floral design, which is destroyed by the very act of passing over it. The flowers that are to be employed are picked beforehand and kept in water in the dark; in the morning their petals are stripped off and placed in large baskets, those of each flower separately—the white acacia, the golden broom, the red rose and poppy, the blue chicory, the green box and laurel, and the dark violets. At the same time the designs that are to be used are marked on the streets with chalk and are divided into sections, each section alloted to a different artist. In the afternoon the baskets of flowers are brought out and the elaborate designs are filled out with their various colors, in readiness for the evening procession.

Similar carpets are also used to decorate some of the churches of Torre del Greco, near Naples, but here the greater part of the decoration is painted on the floor. Only the borders are carried out in flower petals.

In Austria. Picturesque Corpus Christi processions take place in many parts of Austria. The most impressive celebrations are held on boats on the Traunsee and Hallstättersee. In each case, a decorated boat bears the Holy Sacrament across the lake, followed by a procession of boats with worshippers.

In England. The Amen Corner is not, as many people believe, a corner in the front of the church where the most vocal and pious of the brethren sit and shout their agreement with the preacher's pronouncements. It is, rather, a street corner in the city of London.

In the days before the Reformation there was always a procession in London on Corpus Christi Day, and all points along the route still bear names that indicate the progress of the procession. Beginning at Cheapside, the clergy moved down the street chanting the *Lord's Prayer*, which in Latin is called the *paternoster* ("Our Father"). The street is still called Paternoster Row. Over the years they learned to time their singing so exactly that they always finished their prayer and sang "Amen" just as they reached a certain corner. Naturally that corner came to be called "Amen Corner." Then, as they began the *Ave Maria*, they turned the corner and proceeded down another street which to this day is known as Ave Maria Lane.

CORPUS CHRISTI IN MEXICO

Mexican cities and towns still adhere to the outdoor celebration. One of the picturesque aspects of the festival is the *reposiar*, small altars which the villagers set up along highways, particularly at crossroads. These shrines are covered with hand-embroidered or lace-trimmed altar cloths and decorated with candles, flowers, and garlands of greens. Canopies of interwoven green branches give the altars the appearance of woodland chapels. The priest gives his benediction to these places of worship as he makes his village rounds.

The quaint custom of having a "mock market" set up along the path of the procession is for the benefit of the children. Each occupation manufactures miniature objects of his trade and displays them in various stalls; builders make doll houses, restaurant keepers set up small tables and serve small portions in miniature dishes, weavers offer tiny blankets and belts for sale, and farmers exhibit seeds of what they grow. Bakers make inch-size bread which the children use for money, and when they ask "How much?" a reduction in price is given!

SHAVUOT (FEAST OF WEEKS)
A FESTIVAL OF THE FIRST FRUITS

Shavuot, or Feast of Weeks, is a Jewish festival that is celebrated at the same time as Whitsunside—seven weeks after Passover. It arrives just as spring is about to turn into summer and is a holiday of threefold joy and pleasure. It was first celebrated in biblical days at the conclusion of the grain harvest when the Hebrews brought their first fruits to Mount Zion. In later years,

70

Shavuot was identified as a holiday commemorating the revelation of the Ten Commandments to Moses at Sinai.

It was customary to bring to the temple at Jerusalem as an offering to God two loaves of bread baked from the new wheat crop. From Shavuot to Sukkot, an unending parade of Jewish families would come to the temple with their harvest in thanksgiving. Today, in the synagogue, it is customary to read from the Book of Ruth, which tells, in part, how the Hebrew farmer was instructed by God to leave a corner of his field and the gleanings for the poor.

As the holiday became recognized to be the time of giving, it attained a more spiritual nature. Thus on the eve of Shavuot many people observe the holiday by reading the Bible and studying other religious books.

One of the prettiest Shavuot customs is the decorating of the house with plants and flowers. The greens recall the mountains of Sinai, where the Commandments were given, as well as the fruits of the ancient harvest festival.

PROCESSION OF THE SWALLOW—MARCH 1

In Greece, the most striking custom of March 1 is the "Procession of the Swallow." In the villages and towns two children fill a basket with ivy leaves; they pass a rod through the handle, and at the end of the rod they attach the "swallow," a wooden effigy of a bird, around whose neck little bells are hung. The two children go from house to house with the basket, singing: A swallow came to us—she sat on a bough and sweetly sang—March, good

March—and ugly February,—what if you grow sour, what if you grow cross;—there will soon be a smell of summer—and even if you bring snow—it will soon be spring.—And you, good wife,—go down to the cellar—bring up some speckled eggs—bring a little hen—bring a little bun.—Come in, Joy.—Come in, Health—for the master, for the mistress—for the children and the parents—and all the good relatives.

The housewife takes a few ivy leaves from the basket and puts them in the nest of her hen, so that she may lay more eggs. She gives the children a few eggs and they move on to another house. Ivy is a symbol of evergreen vegetation and it is believed to have the power to transfer health to hens and other animals.

HINA—MATSURI—DOLL FESTIVAL

Peach blossoms are usually in full bloom in Japan on the day of the Doll Festival, so the third day of the month is also known as the Peach Festival. The girls put their ceremonial dolls in a special room for friends and relatives to admire. The dolls are shown for only one day then packed away in big boxes until next year's festival.

Peach blossoms, which are Japanese symbols of happiness in marriage, are arranged carefully around the dolls. These flowers also stand for feminine qualities of mildness, softness, and peacefulness that all girls hope to have by the time they are married.

International Women's Day, celebrated March 7 chiefly in socialist countries, is the counterpart of Mother's Day or St. Valentine's Day. There is no commercial institution in Russia comparable to printed greeting cards bearing sentimental messages. Instead, sentiment is commonly expressed by sending flowers. On this day the price of flowers soars on the free market with a single gladiola forty-five cents in the afternoon.

Official greetings to women everywhere are conveyed by red and white banners on buildings, and through the press, radio, and television. In 1970, the liberally oriented theater in Moscow scheduled Gorky's "Mother" for the evening performance, and *Pravda*, the Communist party newspaper, noted that there were 3,925 women with the title Hero of (the) Socialist Labor and 91 were Heros of the Soviet Union.

Pravda also promised working women that the party planned to "free women from many household matters." "All the flowers today are for you . . . women!" *Pravda* said. But the paper's message reach many Soviet women while they were hard at work in their homes and factories.

ST. PATRICK'S DAY

St. Patrick's Day, March 17, is not only a great day for the Irish, but for the people of other countries as well. Americans, especially, like to wear a bit of green on this day even though their ancestors never set foot on Irish soil. All over the United States, the day is one of rejoicing and merrymaking, especially in larger cities where the streets take on a green haze and the traditional St. Patrick's Day Parade occurs.

In Ireland, St. Patrick's Day is on the sedate side: loyal sons of Erin may mark the day by singing of the shamrocks, but they also fill the churches and cathedrals, paying homage to the saint whose blessed day it is. County Cork is the center of the shamrock trade in Ireland, and each year several million plants are potted and sent all over the world to be sold on streets and florist shops on March 17.

EGYPT, SHAM AL-NESSIM—THE SMELLING
OF SPRING

On March 21, or on the first beautiful day of spring, everyone in Egypt participates in the happy holiday of Sham al-Nessim. The custom is for the entire family to spend the day out-of-doors enjoying and sniffing the delightful scent of spring. An important feature of the day is to visit the most beautiful spot possible, and this is often a matter for serious discussion between parents and their children. Some families make a trip to an oasis in the desert, some go on an excursion boat up the Nile or to a picnic ground, while others go to beautiful beaches.

The most important part of the holiday for the child is a large lunch prepared particularly for the noonday meal. In the afternoon, there are games, singing, and storytelling. Boys along with their fathers like to try their hand at kiteflying. The holiday offers a special opportunity for everyone to become more aware of the beauty of spring.

DAY OF YOUTH—MARSHAL TITO'S BIRTHDAY

All over the country, on March 25, every Yugoslav youth contributes to the monumental birthday celebration for Marshal Tito, who has turned the occasion into a national festival for youth. Anywhere up to two weeks beforehand, youthful runners set out from remote villages all over the country, bearing messages to Belgrade. Greetings pass from hand to hand, rather as in a marathon race, until they pour by the thousands into Belgrade on an appointed day. Sporting contests, cultural events, and folk dances take place everywhere in the country during this period, culminating in the big festivities in Belgrade itself. The whole operation is an example of teamwork on a national scale.

ALL FOOL'S DAY

April 1 is the day on which practical jokes of the salt-in-the-sugar-bowl type are commonly practiced. The day is widely observed but of obscure origin. Especially typical is the sending of people on fool's errands. April Fool's Day came into common practice in England in the eighteenth century. In Scotland it is called hunting the gowk (cuckoo). In France the person fooled is a *poisson d'avril*. The fooling includes pointless errands, April Fool candy, rubber mice, the pocket book on a string, to fool the unsuspecting.

In Mexico, All Fool's Day falls on December 28 and centers on the borrowing of objects; if anyone is foolish enough to lend, the items borrowed on that day need not be returned. A poem reminding the lender that he has been fooled is sent instead. The day is popular in Italy, Spain, Portugal, Sweden, Germany, and Norway. In the latter two, it is celebrated on the first and last days of April.

SHIOHI-GARI—SHELLFISH GATHERING, APRIL 4

On April 4, Japanese have a holiday known as Shiohi-gari, or Shellfish Gathering. It is a pastime enjoyed by young and old alike. As far as one can see, the beaches at ebb tide will be alive with holidaymakers, colorfully clothed. Many large parties in boats decorated with white and red bunting arrive at the selected spot for shellfish gathering and wait until they are stranded on the sea bottom by the ebbing tide. When the party is thus provided with a base, clams gathered are often cooked on the spot for lunch. If the party has a streak of bad luck, fishermen living along the coast have large stocks for sale and the people usually buy a bag or two to take home.

April 4 is chosen as the date for gathering the shellfish because it is on this date the tide will be at its lowest. The water police often have to call out reserves during the day to prevent possible accidents when daring persons go out too far and are caught by the incoming tide.

HANA MATSURI—BIRTH OF BUDDHA—APRIL 8
IN JAPAN

Hana Matsuri, or Flower Festival, is observed on April 8 in all Buddhist temples throughout Japan to commemorate the birthday anniversary of Gautama Buddha, founder of Buddhism. The feature of the day is the ceremony of bathing Buddha with *amacha* (sweet tea prepared from hydrangea leaves). Millions of people proceed to their neighborhood temples to bathe the image of infant Buddha with the sweet tea. Those who visit the shrine bring fresh flowers, so modern Japanese call it the Flower Festival. Little girls appear with faces powdered white so they will appear clean and fresh to Buddha, and students in special robes carry offerings and chant Buddha prayers.

The highlight of the festival is the procession of Buddhist priests and students of Buddhist schools marching through the principal sections of the cities in costumes of former days. The parade is usually accompanied by a large number of children beautifully decked out in colorful silk kimonos. There are also floats of various kinds, but one of them always has a huge white elephant bearing the image of Buddha. There are no elephants in Japan but there are in India, where Buddha spent most of his life, and the Japanese honor him by having an elephant as his birthday *matsuri*.

An important attaction in Kamakura, Japan, is a great bronze image of Buddha. It may be reached in about fifteen minutes by bus from in front of the Kamakura railway station. It was erected to fulfill his wish, but the statue was not constructed until 1259, or sixty years after his death. It's gigantic dimensions are as follows:

> Circumference, 79'
> Height, 37' 5"
> Length of face, 7' 5"
> Length of eye, 3' 4"
> Length of ear, 6' 3"
> Length of eyebrow, 4' 1"
> Length of nose, 2' 8"
> Length of mouth, 2' 7"
> White spot (silver) between eye brows, 5" in
>   thickness and 6" in diameter.
> Number of curls on the head, 646, each 6"
>   in thickness and 8" in diameter.

Throughout China innumerable temples have been erected to Buddha, and on this "day of remembrance" the *Sutras* are chanted musically with the accompaniment of booming drums, the tinkle of small bells, the thud of wooden fish-heads (symbol of watchfulness as the fish never closes it's eyes) struck with a small stick, the clang of brass cymbols, and a flat metallic plate cut out in flower shapes and struck with a thin iron rod to mark time for the chanters.

The evening before, there is the ceremony of washing images of the gods which takes place once a year. All the statues, whether wood or stone, are carried out into the courtyard and sprinkled with water which must be exceptionally pure. Strips of paper are carefully pasted over Buddhas' eyes so that he cannot see the statues being bathed. He is also blindfolded while the sanctuary is being dusted.

"Washing of Buddhas" are very picturesque because each monastery, glowing with lanterns, appears like a torch against the darkness of night. Outside the entrance gate stand two stone lions, guardians of Buddha. In passing the gate one will notice that all important buildings face south. The first hall of the temple contains gigantic statues of the Four Diamond Kings, two on either side guarding the entrance. In general, they may be taken to represent four seasons or four directions.

In the old days, pilgrims had a special manual for their guidance when visiting various shrines on Buddha's birthday. It included information concerning roads, where "they were to bend the knee and open purse." Every village offered fresh eggs, and bowls of water were set out for thirsty animals. On the mountains a series of little temples marked the regular halts, and in addition, there were open air restaurants where the view inclined weary visitors to sip a cup of tea and eat a bowl of rice. After offering endless prayers and performing numerous rites, the pilgrims lingered on to enjoy the view of the Hun River, then descended the mountain in picturesque procession by the light of torches flaming among the rocks.

78

The birth date of Mohammed is set as April 20, A.D. 571. His birthday is a gay occasion, with processions, booming of cannons, and fireworks as a part of the celebration. Cantatas of the birth and life of the Prophet are sung by professional musicians, as well as at weddings and other occasions of rejoicing. As in all important Muslim festivals, the various sects forget their differences and join together in ceremonial prayer, out-of-doors. Mohammed warned against division among his followers; according to tradition, he said: "My people will be divided into 73 sects. Everyone of these sects will go to Hell except one." The orthodox Moslems believe that they are the one chosen sect.

FIVE PRINCIPAL ISLAM HOLIDAYS

As in all religious festivals (there are five holidays honoring Mohammed), it is necessary to have some coherent idea of their origins and the beliefs upon which they are based.

The religious duties of a Muslim are based upon what were termed by Mohammed the "Five Pillars of Faith." Let us define the Five Pillars since the most important Muslim holidays were designed to fulfill their tenets:

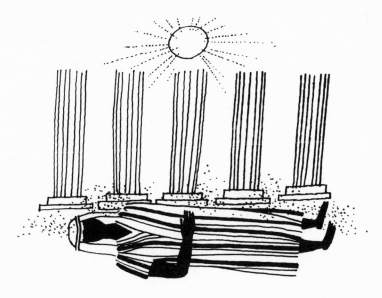

First Pillar of Faith—Mohammed presented to his people the idea that there is no other God but Allah and that Mohammed is the Prophet of Allah. *Laitat-al-Quadr* celebrates the "First Revelation of Mohammed," approximately the twenty-fourth of the tenth Moon.

Second Pillar of Faith. The duty of a Moslem is to worship the One God in prayer five times each day. Thus, five times a day 300 million Muslims, bowing in prayer, face toward Mecca, a small oasis town in the vast Arabian desert.

Third Pillar of Faith. The duty of every Muslim is to distribute alms and to help the needy. There is no organized charity to provide for the poor but a man should give one-tenth of his income in alms. *Ide Ahha*—Feast of Sacrifice—is held in honor of the Third Pillar, approximately the tenth of the twenty-first Moon.

Fourth Pillar of Faith. It is the duty of every True Believer to keep the Fast of Ramdan, which takes place in the fall. Id-il-Fitr—End of Ramdan—is the greatest Muslim festival of the year and is celebrated the first of the tenth Moon.

Fifth Pillar of Faith. It is the duty of every Muslim to make the pilgrimage to Mecca at least once in a lifetime, if possible. *Al-Isra* celebrates the "Vision of Journey of Mohammed to Mecca from Jerusalem,"—approximately the fifteenth of the eighth Moon.

TURKEY, CHILDREN'S DAY—APRIL 23

Children's Day is a patriotic holiday in Turkey and serves two purposes. It commemorates the inauguration of the Grand National Assembly on April 23, 1923, and calls attention to the fact that children symbolize modern, democratic Turkey. It emphasizes Turkey's intention to look to the future and not to the past. There are all manner of modern enjoyments, too, for the youngsters of Turkey that day. Movies are free, taxi drivers give them free rides, and a few merchants distribute free ice cream and candy. Elective representatives from schools in Ankara visit the president, who receives them in company with his wife and children and presents them with small gifts. Other young people take over the duties of civic officials for the day, and there are dances and parties in public places and private homes throughout the nation.

St. George, the knight on the white horse, is one of the most popular saints, and his feast is kept on April 23 throughout the world. More than any other saint, perhaps, St. George is the incarnation of the ideal hero of antiquity, and several ancient legends have caused him to be associated with demigods and heroes of Greek mythology. The miraculous exploit of St. George —how he slew the dragon and rescued the princess thrown as a prey to the beast in order to let the waters of the city run free— is from a translation into English by Claxton.

The shepherds of the Alps pay St. George special homage. The reason for this is probably that his name day coincides with the time when shepherds and their flocks move up to the mountain pastures. Every year on St. George's Day lambs are sacrificed or offered to the church by all those who have made the Saint a vow in the hope of finding their lost sheep, or who have invoked his help in an hour of need.

In England. St. George was made patron saint of England about 1344. His day is marked by the rose and his flag, which is the banner of the Church of England—a red cross with a white background. The order of St. Michael and St. George holds an impressive service in St. Paul's Cathedral in London on April 23. The members wear vivid blue capes lined with scarlet.

In America a Sons of St. George Society was organized in Philadelphia in 1772. Membership was restricted to natives of "that part of Great Britain called England." Early members included Robert Morris, Benjamin Franklin, and William Penn. The Society holds annual dinners on April 23 in cities all over America.

In Greece, the exploits ascribed to the Saint, and the time of year at which he is feasted, have lead those who honor his memory to hold various athletic games on his name day. The games held are characteristic of the traditional athletic spirit of the Greeks.

The festivities last three days. On the first day the service is followed by "the race of the old men." The old men of the village go to a sharp slope covered with loose stones and race each other barefoot to the top; a lamb or a ram is placed at the summit of the slope for the winner; it is offered by the sheep owners to bring good luck to their flocks. The second day is devoted to a jumping contest, and the third to wrestling matches and putting the weight. The contests are followed by dancing and a procession headed by the icon of the Saint.

On the island of Lemnos the games also include horseraces. After the service, a number of horses, mounted by young men, race toward a large loaf of bread placed at a distance. The horseman who gets it must cut it up into slices and share it with the other competitors. At Basta, in Messinia, the church committee awards prizes: a saddle, a set of harness, or a gun. Sometimes the winner is the man who has defeated three consecutive opponents.

In Syria, St. George has numerous shrines in different parts of the country. One of the most important is a monastery at Humevia, near Tripoli, where both Christians and Moslems make annual pilgrimages and perform sacred vows before the same saint. This is the scene of the great folk festival attended by hundreds of devout worshippers from many different parts of Syria. According to tradition, St. George killed the dragon at Lydd, or, according to another tradition, at Beirut.

In Russia this festival honors the patron of the Military Order of St. George's Cross. The day is observed with special services in the churches and reunion of military officers or recipients of the St. George's decoration. Dinners and celebrations are held for military men of all rank.

8. LATE SPRING FESTIVALS

A springtime festival is an occasion to make merry and to welcome outdoor play. Every country the world over greets the coming of spring in its own way and at different times of the year. In the north, spring festivals are celebrated during the first two weeks of May, while in the Middle East spring comes as early as February. Most Europeans and Americans have always regarded May 1 as being the unofficial beginning of spring.

MAY DAY CELEBRATIONS

The beautiful springtime festival of May Day is observed in every nation, each according to its own customs and traditions. In most countries on May 1 a new life begins for both nature and man. But in the Soviet Union, Japan, and the Philippine Islands, labor unions stage demonstrations in the larger cities on that day. They mobilize factory workers, office clerks, and students for the annual May Day Parade, which lasts throughout the day, with placards and flags of all shapes, singing songs of labor which are virtually a battle cry against capitalists. In Moscow, the May Day Parade is essentially a military one, displaying hundreds of tanks, guns, aeroplanes, and latest weapons of war.

May Day is more important in northern Europe than in warmer

countries farther south. People grow tired of snow and ice and short winter days to which May Day signifies an end. The people of Belgium welcome spring with parades and fairs. Holland celebrates with tulip festivals, and in Switzerland people offer up special May Day prayers. In France the people buy flowers at sidewalk stands. They wear them and give them to their friends for luck.

May Day has always been a popular children's holiday in England. In some villages boys and girls still gather around a may pole and grownups perform the old traditional dances called "Morris dances." Men wear broad red sashes across their chests and hats decorated with bells and ribbons. In some towns they form teams and dance up one side of the street and down another with crowds cheering them on.

SINGING IN THE MAY

A traditional custom of "Singing in the May" early in the morning of May 1 is still practiced in parts of England. The British Broadcasting Company was forced to 'Sing in the May" after 10 A.M. for the benefit of late risers, but at Oxford University a ceremony takes place early, before morning classes are scheduled. A student choir sings May songs from the top of a high tower and hundreds of students gather below to listen. Some stand on a bridge over a river that flows past the tower and others sit in small flat boats called "punts."

As the last song ends, bells ring out and this is a signal for "punt scuttling" among the boats on the river. Students in the craft are armed with long poles with which they try to "scuttle" each other. The fun continues until only one punt remains afloat and is acclaimed the victor.

HANGING MAY BASKETS

The custom of hanging May baskets became popular in the United States in the nineteenth century and is still enjoyed by children today. They like to make their own baskets by weaving strips of colored paper, then decorating them with lace-paper doilies and ribbons. The traditional filler would be: a piece of

candy, a handful of posies, a verse, the name of the person to whom it is sent.

The basket must be hung on a friend's front door in the dusk so the child can scurry away before he is caught. Many baskets are delivered to children and to friends who are ill, to veterans' hospitals, and to the aged who are confined to their homes.

On May Day at Wellesley College the senior girls have a hoop-rolling contest. They put on their graduation caps and long black gowns, which sometimes get caught in their hoops. According to college legend, the winner of the race will be the first to marry.

TREE PLANTING CEREMONIES

Arbor Day was first started in the United Sates in 1872 by a man named J. Sterling Morton. He noticed soil in Nebraska getting dryer and blowing away and he persuaded state officials to have trees planted in barren areas. More than one million trees were planted in the first year. Nebraska became known as the tree-planting state and each year, on April 27—the anniversary of Mr. Morton's birth—children plant trees in his memory. Other states adopted the custom of setting aside one day a year for tree planting, which is generally known as Arbor Day. It is celebrated on a day proclaimed by the governor of each state, but the date is always the same for each state. Most schools have tree-planting ceremonies, and more recently, the trees are planted on the edges of parks or outskirts of cities to become sanctuaries later on for birds.

Birthday Trees. In some countries a birthday tree is planted on the day a child is born, to bring good luck all through his life. The tree is tended carefully because its growth is supposed to foretell the way the child will grow. If the tree thrives, the child will thrive and have good fortune; if the tree should be cut down or wither and die, then the child may become injured and perhaps die. This custom is still followed in country districts in some parts of Europe, especially in Germany. In Switzerland, a pear tree is often planted for a girl, an apple tree for a boy.

Alm Tree. Many a mosque in Palestine has in its courtyard a fig tree whose fruit is for the needy. The poor have the same rights as the birds to eat, but they may eat but not carry the fruit away. Often there is an inscription by an early Moslem writer: "Prayer carries us half way to God; fasting brings us to the door of His palace; alms giving procures for us admission."

Ching Ming ("Bright and Clear") is the chief spring festival in China and lasts for one day only. The celebration begins at daybreak and ends at sundown. It is also called *Chih Shu Chieh*, or "Tree Planting Festival," otherwise, Arbor Day. In years gone by, the emperor or his representative planted trees in the palace grounds on the day of the festival, but now the ceremony is performed by the president of the republic or his representative, and the planting is done in some public place, not on the palace grounds.

The principal ceremony of the day for the Chinese people themselves is the visiting of family graves, to plant trees on them in order to secure permanent possession. If a tree grows on a grave, the keeper of the grounds cannot claim it. The only plant permitted for general grave decoration is the willow. One still sees willow branches stuck in grave mounds because they have a mystical connection with the spring festival.

87

Many towns and communities all over the world hold spring festivals in honor of certain flowers or blossoming trees. The time of year (day or week) of the festival varies from year to year, depending on whether spring arrives early or late.

Three Apple Blossom Festivals
United States, Shenandoah Valley

In 1924 W. A. Ryan, of Winchester, Virginia, conceived the idea of holding an apple blososm festival in the Shenandoah Valley where hundreds of thousands of barrels of apples are grown every year. Winchester became headquarters for the festival, which takes place about three days before the first Sunday in May. Thousands of tourists drive up and down the valley to view the hundreds of apple orchards in full bloom.

On the first day of the festival a queen, known as Queen Shenandoah, is crowned. Young women from neighboring schools and colleges form the court of the queen, which includes a crown bearer, train bearers, and maids of honor. The chief event of the second day is a grand parade, called "Trail of the Pink Petals." It includes, besides the queen and her attendants, floats reviewing history of the valley. Other events during the festival are an art exhibit, apple-pie-baking contest, square dancing, and coronation ball.

United States, Wenatchee Valley

The most ambitious apple blossom festival is held in Wenatchee, Washington, which is situated on the Columbia River about a hundred miles from the Grand Coulee Dam. The date varies from mid-April to early May and is set by a committee, known as the "Three Wise Men," who forecast the time when the trees are expected to be in full bloom. People come from far and near to admire the beautiful scenic effects of the blooming orchards against a dramatic background of mountains and spring sky. A legend is associated with the festival that Peter Pan visits the Wenatchee Valley each year and sweeps it clean in preparation for the lovely spectacle of the blooming trees.

As with all festivals, a queen is crowned who is followed in a parade with bands and numerous beautifully decorated floats. In true Western style, the festivities of the week include cookouts, square dancing, horse shows, rodeos. Apples were first shipped from this area in 1902, and today Wenatchee calls itself "The Apple Capital of the World."

Canada, Annapolis Valley

Since 1930, Americans and people from other countries have been trekking to the Grand Pré Area of Nova Scotia around the last week in May to enjoy the Annapolis Valley Blossom Festival. About that time of year the delicately scented blossoms of the estimated one million apple trees provide a backdrop for the coronation of the festival queen, a parade, barbecue, and dances. This is the same Grand Pré that was the home of the Acadians whom Longfellow immortalized in his poem "Evangeline."

Japan, Hana-mi, or Cherry Viewing

With the advent of March the minds of the Japanese people turn naturally to the thought of cherry blossoms and the anticipation of celebrating the season with the time-honored custom of cherry viewing. As the month wears on, the *Hana-mi*, or "cherry viewing," becomes the talk of the hour. Operators of restaurants and food shops at flower resorts prepare for gay parties of flower viewers in colorful attire as they will arrive in constant streams from cities in all parts of the county. It is a time for gaiety and merrymaking, and the whole day is spent singing, dancing, and feasting under the cherry blossoms.

Until a few decades ago, the Japanese went flower viewing according to the custom of old Japan. Take, for instance, the flower viewing at Ueno Park in Tokyo, one of the most noted cherry resorts in the capital. In former days the holidaymaking at this resort was an elaborate and luxurious affair, young girls of wealthy families trying to outshine one another by dressing in their best holiday kimonos. Parties of cherry-blossom viewers arrived in the park in the morning and went about the task of establishing quarters for the day, each one spreading its mats and red blankets under cherry trees in bloom and hanging broad-striped curtains, bearing the family crest, to screen the place off from the others. Some of the parties stretched ropes from tree to tree around their respective quarters and hung brilliant cloaks and kimonos over the line to serve as curtains.

The matted and blanketed ground thus set off by curtains served as dining room and stage, for after feasting, the members of the parties exchanged greetings and visits with their neighbors, or whiled away the day in merrymaking, dancing, and singing, to the twang of the *shimisen*.

Holland, Tulip Festival

Holland is one of the greatest exporters of bulbs and flowers and the Tulip Festival helps to dramatize their product for the benefit of tourists. The most spectacular staging for the festival can be seen at Hillegom, Lisse, and Sassenheim, usually during the last week in April and the first week in May. The Sunday between the two weeks, when the blooms are at their best, is called "Bulb Sunday"; it is the day when everyone goes to the tulip fields in cars, bicycles, and on foot. People also buy enormous bunches of flowers at roadside stands for only a few cents. This is the time, too, when the contests of flower mosaics are held, and also when the tulip rally and auto race take place.

CHINA, LI CH'UN—SPRING OX

Li Ch'un is a Chinese festival heralding the beginning of spring. Its main feature is a most unusual procession including dancers, singers, and musicians, headed by a huge spring ox and his driver. Both the animal and man are made of stiff paper painted in five colors—red, black, white, green, and yellow. They represent the Five Elements of Nature which are metal, wood, fire, water, and earth.

When these images are being prepared for the approaching festival, a careful examination under official direction is made of the newly issued Almanac and the effigies are dressed up in accordance with the warnings of the publication. Hence the people who go to watch the procession are informed of the agricultural prospects for the coming year.

If they see the head of the ox is painted yellow, they know great heat is foretold for the coming summer; if it is green, there will be much sickness in the spring; if red, there will be a drought; if black, there will be much rain; if white, there will be high winds and storms. The Mêng Shan, or spirit driver, is also a silent prophet of the season. If he wears a hat, there will be rain. Shoes similarly indicate very heavy rain; absence of shoes, drought; abundance of body clothing, cold weather; lightness of clothing, great heat. Finally, a red belt worn by him indicates much sickness and many deaths; a white one, general good health.

In front of their houses people stick in the ground a large piece of hollow bamboo with chicken feathers in it. As the feathers fly upward on the first breeze, everyone knows that spring has actually come!

INDIA, MASI MAGHAM

Masi Magham is a festival Hindus observe in February or March when the moon is full. They come to Kumbakonam, in Southern India, to bathe in the Maha-Magha tank, which is considered to be the most sacred of all holy waters, because the

91

waters of nine holy rivers are said to be present there: Ganga (Ganges), Yumma (Jvmva), Godavari, Saraswati, Narmada, Cauvery, Kumari, Payoshni, and Sarayu. Consequently, people from all parts of India gather here to bathe in the sacred tank and become purified of their sins. Over the years as many as sixteen elaborate temples have been constructed on its banks.

The Masi Magham festival is observed every twelve years, but a small festival or celebration takes place every spring. Gifts are presented by one individual to another, or to a large number of people, or in support of charitable institutions already in existence. Of many ways of helping people by gifts, the one by the name of *Tulabhara* is the most unusual. Only the very rich can adopt this mode of giving, as it consists of weighing oneself against gold and and distributing the precious metal to the deserving poor. At times the gold weighed against is used for renovating the sixteen temples or building new ones.

The origin of the custom of flying kites is traced to the Erioku era (A.D. 1558–1569) when the retainer of the lord Iio, master of Hamamatsu Castle, congratulated his lord on the birth of his first son and heir by flying a large kite with the name of the newborn child written on it.

May 1 to 5 are the dates of the kite-flying contest in Hamamatsu. During the five days, men in each ward of different cities assemble on the military parade ground with their kites to stage the so-called "kite battle." The kites flown are usually two to four yards square, a convenient size for the battle.

The contestants are all expert kite fliers, making their kites sail right and left or dip or rise, with remarkable speed. Each party has a cutting contrivance attached to a certain section of the string near the kite. When the battle begins between two parties, each makes all possible effort to bring his kite to an advantageous position from which he can cut the enemy's kite adrift by severing it's string.

MEXICO, DAY OF HOLY CROSS

In Mexico on May 3, Day of Holy Cross, mountain, roadside, and village crosses are adorned with flowers and there are many fiestas to miraculous crosses over the country. Civil authorities come with new crosses to replace old ones. They march past the churches first, accompanied by musicians playing a harp, guitar, and drum. The crosses are dressed in new clothes, kerchiefs, and ribbons.

Also on the Day of Holy Cross, the patrons of masons set up on every building job new crosses, which are decorated with flowers and colored streamers. The bigger the job, the more elaborate the cross. At noon all work is stopped; the men surround the cross, drink *copitas tequila* or any other liquor and shoot off firecrackers.

BIRD WEEK

United States

Audubon societies have spread the idea of setting aside a week each year to honor birds. The societies are named for John James

Audubon, who lived from 1785 to 1851, and they honor his birthday, April 26. In some states, Audubon Day and Arbor Day are celebrated together and trees are planted for bird sanctuaries, where school children can care for the birds and study their habits.

Japan

Bird Week in Japan begins May 10. The celebration is under the auspices of the Education Ministry to encourage wild birds which feed on insects harmful to farm crops. There are many lectures, and high schools in various parts of the country win special prizes for meritorious service they render, such as providing a large pine forest for nesting birds.

The movement has become popular because of the fact that during the war in the Pacific immense quantities of trees were felled to feed various munition factories, thus destroying a great many bird nests and killing the young. As a result, parasitic insects on growing trees have become widespread, causing considerable damage to rural districts.

Cormorant Fishing—Japan
Season Begins May 11

Ukai, or fishing *ayu,* a kind of fresh-water trout, by means of cormorant, on the Nagara River, some two hundred and fifty miles west of Tokyo, has been celebrated for centuries as one of Japan's national features.

No method of catching fish is as novel and fascinating as the one practiced by using trained cormorants, on a dark night, by the light of a fire burning out over the water from the fishing boat. A cormorant fisherman usually operates with a flock of several black birds tied to a string. He manipulates the strings with remarkable skill, enabling the birds to rush back and forth after the fish that gather around the vessel, attracted by the light of the bonfire. The cormorants swallow the fish they catch, but rings on the lower parts of their necks prevent their prey from going down into their stomachs. After several fish are caught, the black birds are made to give them up.

The master of the birds must handle deftly his twelve strings that let the birds dash hither and yon as they will, and especially he must watch for the moment when any of his flock is about to gorge. When this happens, the master must shorten the one line, squeeze out the fish with his right hand, and start the bird off on a fresh foray.

Ugai has been practiced in Japan as early as the tenth century, and it is a custom among the fishermen to offer the first catch of the season to the Emperor.

Purple Spring in Peru (Lima)

Springtime comes in October in Peru, when the sun begins to break through the winter clouds and the Jacaranda trees are in bloom. It is called the purple month because devotees of Señor de los Milagrous wear purple—the men wear purple bands on their arms and the women dress in purple robes with a white cord around their waists.

Señor de los Milagrous was a nameless Negro artist who painted an image of Christ on an adobe wall of the brotherhood to which he belonged. In 1655, a violent earthquake occurred in that section of Lima, and many buildings were destroyed and lives lost. Only the wall with the image of Christ remained. Again, in 1687, a more violent earthquake took place and this time almost the whole city was demolished and over a thousand lives were lost.

In desperation, the wall with Señor de los Milagrous' painting was taken on procession for three days and the earth stopped shaking. Since that time, two processions carrying the Señor's painting take place in Lima every October.

The original piece of wall, with the image of Christ, is housed in the small church of Las Mazarenas in the center of Lima. A copy of the painting has been made for the processions. All during October the church is filled with flowers and huge candles adorned with purple ribbons. The Novena begins on October ninth and continues until the first procession starts.

Before the procession gets into the church, distinguished guests in Lima are honored by invitation to carry the litter. The devout of all classes and colors show their gratitude by wearing purple, the color of the Negro brotherhood that still claims the right to plan the fiesta, taking care of everything and spending money on the parade. Some of the Negros walk backward in order not to turn their back on the Señor. Thousands of men and women follow—rich and poor, white and mestizo, Indian and Orientals— all barriers of caste and color forgotten as they unite in singing special chants and prayers. When the procession reaches the Plaza de Armas, the president comes out on his balcony and remains kneeling until the image passes.

9. SUMMER FESTIVALS

Punctuality day, or time-observance day, an annual national campaign urging the people to realize the value of keeping correct time, falls on June 10 under the auspices of the Federation for the Improvement of Living Conditions. June 10 was selected for the campaign because it was the day on which the Emperor Tenchi, thirty-eighth Emperor of Japan (A.D. 663–671)), ordered the hours announced by sounding temple bells and drums.

According to the Nihongi, one of the ancient records of the period A.D. 673 to 721, the water clock, a device to measure time by the amount of water leaking out of a vessel, was first made in Japan by the Emperor Tenchi, when he was still Crown Prince. It is not known whether he invented this method of measuring time or worked it out after a foreign model, but the practice of observing time in Japan as early as the seventh century is significant and worth commemorating.

Lecture meetings held on this day emphasize the importance of keeping time punctually. The Federation honors many persons, recommended by local governments, who have kept correct time and rendered meritorious service for the furtherance of the cause.

In Tokyo, the organization used to mobilize a number of watch-makers and station them at important sections of the city such as, for instance, in front of Tokyo Central Railway Station to offer pedestrians free service for adjusting the "fast and slow" controls of their time pieces.

In former days—and even today—the Japanese were careless about keeping time. It was often the case that the starting time of a meeting was not announced at all, and functions began when the promoter was ready to begin. A few hours one way or the other was not embarrassing either to the hosts or guests, so the Federation decided to do something about it.

ST. JOHN'S DAY—JUNE 24

St. John the Baptists' birthday is undoubtedly one of the most important June festivals in many parts of the world. This day has been given various names according to the beliefs and cus-toms connected with it in each area. The most common appella-tion is St. John the Diviner, because of the various divinatory customs proper to this day. In other areas it is known as the feast of St. John, Bearer of Brightness, because of the bonfires lighted in the streets or the fields on the eve of the feast. In other places, again, it is called the feast of St. John of the Solstice, because this feast day coincides with the summer solstice, and various customs have to do with the longest day of the year.

Since pagan times, Midsummer Eve has been the night of rejoicing and merrymaking over the return of summer. In many villages it is believed that on St. John's Day the "sun quivers, or turns, or grows dim." For this reason the inhabitants rise early to see the sun turning like a "'windmill" or a "wheel," as they say. They stay up all night in groups, spending the long hours dancing, eating, and drinking until the sun comes up. A tradi-tional type of winding dance, imitating the "turning of the sun," was danced on this occasion.

A typical custom on St. John's birthday is the lighting of bon-fires. They are lighted on mountain tops, along streams, in the middle of streets, and in front of houses. One person may be seen jumping over the fire, while others may take off their shoes and walk over the coals when they are burned out to prove they have faith in St. John and will not be burned. According to tradition, the grain will grow as high as one can leap over the St. John fires.

ST. JOHN'S DAY CELEBRATIONS
Estonia, Laulupidu—Singing Festival

Every fifth year (as in 1958, 1963, 1968), Estonians hold their great national singing festival on St. John's Day. Estonian representatives come to Tallin from America, Latvia, Finland, Lithuania, and other countries to participate in this festival of national folk music. Visiting choirs of many nationalities attend as delegates and learn to sing some of the native Estonian songs. All choir members dress in folk costumes of their particular locality.

Scandinavian Countries

St. John's bonfires are built on heights and mountains. These fires made of logs and tar-soaked barrels may be seen for several miles. Young people, singing the old folk songs of their native valleys, go out on the water in gaily decked boats and watch the burning bonfires which are reflected a hundred times in the clear water of the fjords and lakes.

Greece

A striking custom that was to be found in earlier times in Greece, and is still practiced in some rural villages on St. John's Day, is a procession of boy and girl masqueraders. They are escorting the *Kalinitsa*, that is to say the most beautiful girl in the neighborhood. On the eve of the feast all the boys and girls gather at the *Kalinitsa's* house and dress her up as a bride. Four girls help her to dress, pin on her veil, and hang a garland of flowers around her neck; she is also given a bunch of flowers to hold. The procession is then formed, headed by a young boy holding a rod. He is followed by the *Kalinitsa*, behind whom in turn march four "ladies in waiting" and a little girl holding an open parasol over the *Kalinitsa's* head. Twelve other girls walk

99

at her side, and the procession is completed by a group of boys also carrying rods. The parade goes around the village singing: "My beautiful Kalinista, my young bride—my mother sent me to the well for water—for cool water—to water the sweet basil."

If two processions meet at a crossroad, each parasol bearer lowers her parasol over the bride's face so that the two *Kalinitsas* will not set eyes on each other. Next day the children gather at the *Kalinitsa's* house, bringing trays of food and sweets.

Canada

St. John's Day is celebrated all over French Canada. In country parishes there are usually races, games, candy and other good things for sale. Montreal has the most spectacular parade, which moves along one of the principal streets from which all traffic is barred for a time. The most important feature of the parade is a float on which rides a little boy dressed as a shepherd of old, representing St. John as a child, and with him on the float is a pet lamb, all woolly white with a ribbon and bow around it's neck. Great crowds watch the parade and cheer little St. John and his lamb.

100

Mexico

Diade de San Jaun—St. John's Day in Mexico—has to do with St. John, the saint of waters, and is honored in every town and hamlet in the republic. Since St. John is said on this day to preside over the waters, people adorn their wells and fountains with flowers, tapers, and gay festoons, and wash in streams and rivers. At midnight they begin to bathe to the gay music of the village band. In rural districts the festival is observed with bathing, eating, dancing, and music.

In Mexico City and other metropolitan centers, the celebration takes place in the fashionable bathhouses. Diving and swimming contests, band music, flowers, and general gaiety characterize the scene.

Denmark

All over Denmark, on June 23, every Dane takes part in the national rejoicing during one of the longest days of the year. Along the coast, particularly north of Copenhagen, thousands of bonfires fling their sparks into the long twilight. A "witch is burned too in some places, symbolical of the arrival of summer."

Brazil

One of the most important festivals in Brazil begins on St. John's Day and lasts until St. Peter's Day on June 29. According to Roman Catholics in Brazil, Mary the mother of Jesus went to visit her cousin Elizabeth, who promised to notify Mary of the birth of her child by building a bonfire in front of her house and setting off fireworks. Thus, on June 23, the day on which John the Baptist's birthday is celebrated, almost all Catholics in Brazil build large bonfires, of pieces of dry wood, in front of their homes. The father lights the fire at six o'clock in the evening. All the family and friends gather around it, telling fortunes, singing and dancing.

ST. PETER'S DAY—JUNE 29

The Apostle Peter was a fisherman; he is the patron saint of those who make their living from the water. Peter is usually repre-

sented as an old man, bald, but with a flowing beard, dressed in a white mantle and blue tunic, and holding a book or scroll in his hand. He was first called Simon, but Jesus changed his name. Jesus said to Peter, "Thou art Peter, and upon this rock I will build my church" (Matthew 16:18). Thus Peter became the first Pope.

From early times the Vatican hill in Rome has been pointed out as the place of Pete's martyrdom, and St. Peter's Church houses his tomb. This tomb is the principal shrine in Europe and draws as many pilgrims as the holy places in Jerusalem.

In Belgium, on this saint's day, the farmers used to build bonfires in his memory. Nowadays, on the Sunday following the saint's day, in the seaport villages all the fishermen and others who are in any way exposed to the perils of the sea attend special church services.

In Portugal, St. Peter's Day, or Sâo Pedro, is celebrated with fairs, singing and dancing, and fireworks.

In America, St. Peter's Day is celebrated in Gloucester, Massachusetts, by Italian fishermen. The Roman Catholic church blesses the fishing boats in the harbor and the festival lasts three days. Ever since Colonial times the Gloucester fishermen have been noted for their daring and skill. A famous statue, "Fishermen's Memorial," overlooks the well-protected harbor. The city is decorated with flags and bunting and the Italian-Americans erect elaborate altars in the street where the religious services are held. There are many colorful dances for people to enjoy.

In Italy, fishermen of Baccadasse and others honor their protector. In the daytime they go to church and at night light bonfires. The places where people sit around and eat fish are decorated with branches and flowers and colored lights. The fiesta usually ends with a great display of fireworks.

In Finland, on lake shores and up and down the country, bonfires flicker in the twilight of the brief northern night, while north of the Arctic Circle the sun works tirelessly around the clock. Special late performances are held in open-air theaters in most towns, and dances are arranged in the large hotels.

CH'U YUAN—DRAGON BOAT FESTIVAL

This Chinese festival is celebrated in midsummer during the Fifth Moon. According to popular tradition, the holiday commemorates a high-minded statesman and poet, called Ch'ü Yüan, who, because the people turned a deaf ear to his council jumped into the T'ung Ting Lake clasping a great rock in his arms. The people wept for admiration of his sacrifice and fed rice upon the waters to feed his ghost. One day his ghost appeared on the bank and said: "I have been unable to avail myself of your offerings because of a huge reptile (dragon) which seizes and devours all things that are cast into the waters. I request you therefore bind

103

your offerings in small pieces of silk and bind the same by means of five threads, each being a different color. These the reptile will not dare to touch." This request is the origin of the triangular rice cakes that, nowadays folded in leaves, are still offered at Ch'ü Yüan.

Regattas of dragon boats are a popular amusement where rivers and lakes are numerous. Races sometimes last several days during the Dragon Boat Festival. Thousands of people crowd the shores where mastheads are erected for their convenience. Family picnics on the decks of brightly painted red and purple junks are the order of the day. Suddenly the attention of the crowd is fixed on the starting point of the races between the huge boats, resembling dragons, each over ninety feet long and so gracefully slim that two men are crowded as they sit side by side. High prows are shaped like a dragon's head with open mouth and cruel fangs, and the long body between is gaily painted to represent scales and touched up with brilliant gilding. One man stands in the bow of each boat, as if looking for the corpse of Ch'ü Yüan, and throws his arms about as though casting rice upon the waters. Others wave brilliant flags or beat gongs and cymbals, so that the deafening clamor may frighten away the dragon.

Then the signal is given and the rhythmic splash of two hundred paddles, kept in time of a coxswain with a bright waving banner, sends the dragons with arrow speed through the water.

Bitter rivalry exists between the boats of different guilds, and deafening applause greets the winners, all forming part of an unforgettable spectacle.

Alas! the joy of the Dragon Day sport is often marred by fatal accidents, as owing to their shallowness and their peculiar construction, the dragon boats may capsize, causing loss of life. After dark the dragon boats are often taken down the course again in slow procession and outlined with lanterns. The effect is fairylike in the warm waters alive with phosphorescence. Oars gleam light at each stroke, then suddenly they go out like a blown lamp-flame.

In Oostduinkerke, Belgium, a Shrimp Festival is held early in July. It is the last of Belgium's beaches where one can still see the picturesque custom of shrimping on horseback. Mounted shrimpers drag trawl nets through the water at low tide and, afterward, the freshly boiled shrimps are offered for sale.

JAPAN, NIGHT-SINGING INSECTS—BEGINS JULY 1

Real signs of the advent of summer begins in early July in Japan, when dealers of night-singing insects begin their seasonal business at shrine and temple festivals, displaying tiny bamboo cages of different shapes—the temporary abodes of tiny captives. It is true these insects do not sing, but all make fascinating notes with rhythmic charm of one kind or another; these include crickets, bell insects, and grasshoppers. Fireflies are not musical, but dealers keep them as part of their stock in trade because they are popular for the pale lighted "lanterns" that twinkle in the lower part of the body.

ITALY, FESTA DEL GRILLO—THE CRICKET

In Florence, Italy, the spring fiesta called *Festa del Grillo* takes place on Ascension Day. In the morning, crowds go out into the immense Cascina Public Gardens on the Arno for *grilli*, or "crickets." Formerly people caught them themselves, but now they buy them in tiny wooden or wire cages in which the little fellows are imprisoned with a large lettuce leaf that serves as their food. The whole fiesta is an authentic one, appealing to children. The pretty painted cages, balloons, toys—everything is bright. The Florentines say that if the *grillo* sings soon, it means good luck.

SWITZERLAND, FIRST FRUITS OF THE ALPS

On the fourth Sunday in August, dairymen of Vissoie hold an impressive ceremony at which they present the parish priest with cheeses known as *les prémices des Alpes*, the first fruits of the Alps. Their gifts are made in appreciation of faithful spiritual service the priest has rendered to members of his flock, who annually migrate with their herds to high Alpine pastures.

In early spring the men leave the valley with their animals and dairy equipment and slowly ascend the steep passes to summer huts, perched in the mountains where grass is green and lush. Throughout the season the priest regularly visits the men to read Mass and administer Holy Sacraments. Traditionally, the dairymen dedicate to the priest all the milk the herd yields on the third day after their arrival in the mountains. This milk they make into cheeses, which are large or small according to the number of cattle in the herd.

At the end of the summer, the Justice of Peace of Val d' Anniviers, his assistant and recorder, count, inspect, and weigh the cheeses brought back to Vissoie with the returning herds. The cheeses are then displayed so all can admire them. After High Mass, the fifteen dairymen of the district march in procession to the altar, each man carrying his own cheese. The dairymen stand in line before the altar, with Vissoie's red-and-black robed magistrates on either side, to receive a blessing from the priest. Then the village celebration ends with feasting, toasts, and speeches beneath the chestnut tree in the priest's courtyard.

INDIA, GAYATRI JAPAM

According to the Hindus, it is a scientifically proven fact that sound arranges the atmospheric atoms into definite shapes. Different sounds create different forms, and forms created by sound retain their shapes for longer or shorter periods according to the strength put forward to form them. The sages of old knew this fact and made long and patient experiments, and there is a separate science called *Mantra Sastra* dealing at length with the subject. One of these incantations goes by the name of Gayatri, and every Brahmin is bound to repeat it a number of times at a sitting, thrice every day—early in the morning, at noon, and at time of sunset.

As soon as a form is created it becomes a thing akin to our dynamo, wherein is stored more or less energy both human and divine. The influence radiating from this form shields the individual from whom it originated from all evil influences. If it is surcharged with sufficiently strong energy, it becomes in the hands of its originator a veritable angel, ready to carry out the slightest wish of its master.

Certain occasions are very favorable for creating these forms and surcharging them with energy. The occasions of solar and lunar eclipses are said to be especially favorable for this purpose. The people believe the first day of the dark last month in August is highly conducive for producing maximum effect. So this day of all days—called Gayatri Japam—is selected for the repetition a number of times.

The posture most favorable for the easy assimilation of the sun's energy is supposed to be the one facing the sun in the morning when one performs the repetition of the Gayatri Mantram. To help in the process of keeping the wandering mind more or less fixed, careful counting of the number of times repeated is ordained.

People performing the Gayatri Japam sit in a pure and solitary place where distraction is not possible and repeat the incantations, ten, twenty-eight, or one hundred and eight times, as it suits their convenience and the time at their disposal.

It is laid down that a rosary of twenty-seven, fifty-four, and one hundred and eight beads may be made use of, in keeping count of the Mantram. The rosary may be either of *Rudraksham* or crystal beads. Counting on the fingers and on the joints of the fingers is also resorted to by many.

The Gayatri Japam may be also performed, not with the aim of personal gain, but with the aim of helping the world. Temples and other places where people gather in large numbers are chosen.

AVANI MULAM—HINDU

The religious day of Avani Mulam falls in August or September. There is a myth attached to the origin and importance of this festival.

There once ruled in Madura a king named Aramidhava Pandya,

and during his reign there was a great drought and the river Vaigai was completely dry for a long time. This was because Indra, the God of the celestials, was displeased with the ruler of Madura. One day, all of a sudden, there happened to fall a short, sharp shower, and as a result there was a slight flood in the river. The king wanted to stop the flow of water toward the ocean, so that not a drop of the precious liquid would be lost. This was possible only by arranging a dam across the river. He accordingly apportioned out work on sections of the dam among the people of Madura.

A small portion of the dam was alloted to an old woman whose avocation was to prepare and sell pudding and keep her body and soul together with the small profit she made from her trade. Called upon by the royal ministers to finish her portion, she could not, on account of heavy demands for laborers just then from any quarter of town.

In the guise of a workman with a basket on his head and a spade in his hand, Lord Sundara came to her door. The woman had no money to give the workman, nor did the workman desire to have money paid to him as wages. All he desired was something to satisfy his hunger, and the woman in great glee promised him as much pudding as he could eat.

The pretended workman ate enough to satisfy his hunger and carried with him more for future use. When he came to the spot on the dam alloted to the woman, instead of working, he distributed the pudding to men already at work throwing an embankment across the river. The officials in charge threatened him but work he would not do. When the sun had set, the work of constructing the dam was all over except for the small portion alloted to the woman. Water was escaping through the gap, making it broader and broader each minute, washing away the walls completed by the other workmen.

At this juncture, the king was coming on horseback on a tour of inspection of the work going on. He halted when he came to the gap through which the precious water was running, and blazing with anger asked who the defaulter was. The officials pointed out the lazy workman who had a basket on his head with a hand-ful of earth. As he came near, the king struck him along the back with a cane he carried in his hand.

When the workman received the blow he dropped the small quantity of earth he held in his basket at the gap when, lo! there was no gap to be seen in the embankment. Stupified with aston-ishment at the miracle, the king regained his self-possession and searched for the workman throughout the city but in vain.

By a flash of intuition the king knew that the seeming workman was in reality his patron, Lord Sundara.

Though the Avani Mulam Festival is observed as a festive occa-sion throughout the land, special importance is attached to the center Madura temple, the scene of the incidents. Consequently the celebration is observed there in all its grandeur, with a golden basket and a golden spade. The God Sundara is taken in pro-cession on the festive day from the river Ghat to the temple amidst much rejoicing by the people.

ASSUMPTION DAY—AUGUST 15

The dogma is simply that the body of the Lord's Mother, after her death, was not subjected to the usual disintegrating process but was united with her soul in heaven. Tradition says that after the crucifixion Mary went and lived in the home of the Apostle John, in accordance with arrangements made by Jesus Himself as He hung on the Cross. (John 19:26-27) John's home was in Jeru-salem and it is said that Mary died there.

In Armenia no one eats any of the new crop of grapes until Assumption Day. A tray full of grapes is blessed at the church on this day and after the service everyone is free to enjoy the new fruit. In Belgium, trays of new fruits and grapes are carried in processions from the church to be blessed.

A pleasant Assumption Day custom in some European countries is for every woman named Mary to entertain her friends of the same name. In Italy and Spain there are colorful processions through the streets, and in these countries displays of fireworks are a feature of the day.

Strangest of all Assumption celebrations is perhaps the one at the monastery near Damascus, in Syria, where people come from far and near, bringing offerings of new wheat to the Virgin. What makes it strange is that Mohammedans come too, and join with the Christians in the festival that could have no religious significance for the visitors of another faith.

JAPAN, CLIMBING MT. FUJI
SEASON BEGINS JULY 1

Mt. Fuji may be climbed either by day or night. Many climbers start their journey by night, wishing to see the sunrise from the eighth station, a vantage point from which it may best be viewed. There are six popular routes for the journey up the mountain, and these paths are divided, from the starting point to the summit, into ten "go," or stations. Each station is of unequal distance and is indicated with a stone marker. The stations are provided with stone shelter huts of different sizes with few accommodations. Foreign climbers are advised to provide themselves with food and drink, as the supplies sold enroute may not suit their tastes. During the scaling season, telephone service stations are maintained at five different points on the mountain and there are other services—post office, police station, and hospital supplies.

A ceremony for closing the climbing season is held at Yoshida on or about August 26. This is a fire festival, which takes place in the evening at the foot of the mountain. Thousands of people visit the town to witness the event, in which numerous huge torches erected along the streets are set on fire. The torches are more than ten feet in height and several feet in circumference. Also, each family has a pile of firewood in front of its own house. About half past six, the portable shrine of the Sengen on top of the mountain is borne through the main street. About an hour later, all torches are lit simultaneously. In the meantime, each family sets its woodpile on fire. In a few minutes the torches begin to blaze and crackle until the whole town is converted into a sea of flames, continuing to burn until past midnight.

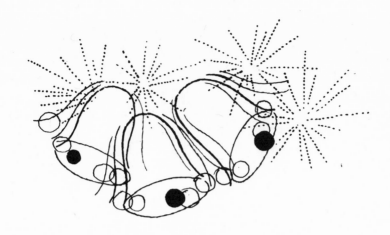

PERU, PROMENADES OF SANTO DOMINGO AND SAN FRANCISCO
AUGUST 4 AND OCTOBER 4

On Santo Domingo's Day, August 4, and again on San Francisco's Day, October 4, a fiesta is held in Lima, Peru. It consists of a charming exchange of courtesies between the two saints and their churches. On each Saint's Day, processions set out from their respective churches and meet on Lima's Plaza de Armas. Each procession includes its own major-domo, music, and members of the congregation.

On the Plaza, under an especially adorned triumphal arch, the images meet. The bearers of the respective litters lower them in majestic reverence to symbolize the historical meeting of the two saints, as church bells ring madly and salvos of fireworks rend the air. On both occasions splendid banquets are offered at monasteries of the saint whose day is being celebrated.

10. FALL FESTIVALS

This festival is based on the Fourth Pillar of Faith laid down by Mohammed, that is, "It is the duty of every True Believer to keep the Fast of Ramadan." Ramadan is a shifting season coming sometimes at the end of summer, sometimes in early fall. It begins when the new moon is first seen and ends with the following new moon. Moslems believe that fasting at Ramadan trains in self-discipline. It quiets the spirit and subdues passions; it gives a sense of unity with Moslems everywhere.

During the Ramadan Fast the faithful spend as much time as possible in the mosque. Each Moslem should hear and read the entire Koran during the month. Lanterns are hung from tops of minarets, and the lamps inside the mosque are lighted for evening prayer. A brilliant illumination of the chief mosques commemorates Mohammed's illumination on the Night of Power.

The Ramadan Fast is observed only during the day, when neither food nor drink may pass into the mouths of the faithful. A cannon or gun announces both the rising and setting sun. One is fired two hours before sunrise to give warning that it is time to prepare the early morning meal. At sunset the well-to-do often eat and drink until "so much of the dawn appears that a white thread may be distinguished from a black; then keep the fast completely until night." (Koran 2: 183).

EID UI FITR—END OF FAST

On the twenty-ninth night of Ramadan, when the new moon appears in the sky, the month of prayer and midday fasting is over and the Breaking of the Fast begins, celebrated by Moslems everywhere—in Jordan, Iraq, Syria, and Morocco. The end of the fast may be announced by the beating of drums, and for three days everyone stops work to celebrate.

On the first morning of Eid Ui Fitr the family, dressed in their best clothes, go to the nearest mosque for prayer and meditation. Then they return home for a feast, their first midday meal for a whole month. There are special foods—*saiwiyan*, thin noodles cooked with milk, sugar, and coconut, and a candy made with ground nuts, sesame seeds, and honey.

In many cities great fairs are opened to mark the end of the Fast of Ramadan. Moslem children often paint their pet sheep in gay colors. A great deal of attention is paid to the children during Eid Ui Fitr. Mothers buy or make them new clothes. All young people go to the village or town square, where they find swings, merry-go-rounds, and perhaps a Ferris wheel. There may also be a puppet show and in the evening fireworks.

As in most Moslem festivals, the final day is spent visiting relatives and friends. The children receive gifts from visitors and also gifts and coins from their parents.

ELEVATION OF THE CROSS—SEPTEMBER 14

This festival is observed by the Greek and Latin churches and is known also as Holy Cross. It commemorates the miraculous vision of the Cross seen by Constantine in A.D. 312, when he was about to fight Maxentius. According to some authorities Constantine himself instituted the feast in honor of the Holy Cross, which appeared in the heavens with the words *In hoc signo visces*—"By this sign you will conquer."

Holy Cross Day is the day on which Greek seamen renounce long journeys at sea, obeying the advice expressed in two popular sayings: "On the day of the Cross, cross your sails and tie your ropes," and "On the day of the Cross, rest in harbour; on St. George's Day rise and set sail again."

JAPAN, BETTARA-ICHI, OR STICKY-STICKY FAIR— OCTOBER 19

The annual fair known as *Bettara*, or "Sticky-Sticky Fair," is one of the most popular events in Tokyo. It is held on October 19 near the Ebisu Shrine to supply the people with articles necessary for the observance of the Ebisu Festival the following day. The fair is well known throughout the city, but most people attending the event are not familiar with the Shrine.

Ebisu is one of the Seven Deities of Good Luck and is the patron deity of the tradesmen. The Ebisu worship is not so popular in this district although Tokyoites love to participite in all such gay and exciting celebrations as the Sticky-Sticky Fair itself.

The Ebisu Festival is observed on October 20 and the Sticky-Sticky Fair is held on the preceding day for the sale of various articles, such as wooden images of Ebisu, luck pieces, artificial red-snappers, *bettara* ("large white pickled radish"), and the like, which are essential for the Ebisu worship. In the course of time, however, the sale of pickled radish has become the feature of the fair.

The sticky-sticky idea dawned on the young men of Tokyo some fifty years ago. They were licensed to have some fun on that day. The Sticky-Sticky Fair received its name from the way the radish, which was pickled with malted rice, was handled by the purchaser in former days. When the pickles were sold, the stall keeper tied them with straw rope and handed them over to his customer. The buyers carried them home by the rope swinging them and shouting "bettara, bettara," so that people might make way for him lest the sticky pickles rub against their holiday clothes.

Young people, who were given to fun and mischief in former days, were delighted with the outdoor sport of swinging sticky-

sticky pickles in a crowd. In those days it was almost certain that screams of young women and children in their holiday clothes at the fair were heard now and then as young rascals with the sticky weapon rushed about shouting "bettara, bettara."

JAPAN, BOOK READING WEEK

In Japan autumn is the season for book reading, time of comfort and delight for booklovers who indulge in quiet reading in the evening after glorious summertime. They are fond of calling autumn "the season to cultivate intimacy with evening light at home for book reading."

Many interesting events are held in all sections of the country for a week beginning October 27, making November 3 middle day —the red-letter day. In Tokyo, one of the outstanding features of the week is a campaign encouraging the people to cultivate the habit of reading good books. The All Japanese Association of Publishers offers a prize for the best selection of ten each of children's books, technical books, and books of general interest published during the past year. Prizes are also offered to publishers who have turned out the largest number of good books during the same period.

EIGHTH MOON FESTIVALS (HARVEST MOON)

China, T'wan Yüan Chieh—Festival of Reunion

T'wan Yüan Chieh, celebrated the fifteenth day of the Eighth Moon, is a festival kept by Chinese women. It commemorates the day when it was made possible for the people to become closely united after one of the most tragic events in China's history.

In the time of the Yüan dynasty (fourteenth century) the Mongols rebelled against China. The rebellion was led by Hu Pi Lieh, and his victorious army advanced against Peking and took the Emperor, Ching Wu Chu, captive to Mongolia. The victors were exceedingly overbearing, causing all to bow to their wills. Up to this time Chinese men had worn their hair long and coiled on top of their heads. Their conquerors now compelled them to shave part of their head and to braid into a queue the hair that remained. The women were made slaves.

The Mongols had been in power for over twenty years when a movement was made against them. By this time the new heir to the Chinese throne had grown to manhood and a council of war was formed to drive out the oppressors. On the fifteenth day of the Eighth Moon the people in each home in the capital were moved by a heaven-sent impulse to get rid of their household tyrants. Though the oppressed were without weapons save their kitchen choppers, hatred strengthened their arms. The surprise attack succeeded and the revolt led to victory. The Chinese heir and his followers came into power, and Mongolia was subjected to Chinese rule again.

T'wan Yüan Chieh is called "Festival of Reunion" in memory of this day when the people became closely united after the years of isolation. It so happens that on this date the moon is full and bright in the heavens. The festival is celebrated by women because there is an old Chinese saying, "Men do not worship the moon, women do not sacrifice to the Kitchen Gods."

Worship of the Moon

The worship of the moon by women is performed the evening of the festival day when the moon is high in the sky, and from nine to eleven o'clock. A table is set in the courtyard of the home; on the table is a picture of the moon, a rabbit, and a pine tree. In front of the picture are placed "moon cakes" (a sweet cake made especially for this festival), several plates of fruit, sometimes some grain, and two beanstalks bearing leaves, this last for the rabbit. All the married women in the home, whose husbands are living, burn incense and bow before the picture on the table. After the worship is over, all members of the household drink wine and eat fruit, and then consume the moon cakes.

Moon Cakes

Moon Cakes (*yüeh ping*) are the distinctive offering of the T'wan Yüan Chieh festival. They are made of grayish (moon-colored) flour and piled thirteen in a pyramid because thirteen

116

represents the months of a complete Chinese year, and likewise, a complete circle of happiness. The cakes also have a deeper meaning. In the fourteenth century, when China was being ruled by the Mongols, these cakes were the means of conveying secret instructions to Chinese patriots who took part in the rebellion. The people were in great despair because of their helplessness till someone hit upon the idea of writing a secret message on little paper squares stuck inside the moon cakes. When sent, as they still are, from neighbor to neighbor and friend to friend, the pastries carried an order for a rising *en masse* at midnight.

Moon Hare

The Moon Hare also appears on every altar and is represented by a special tablet or a little clay figure. Just at the hour when the moon is clear of the treetops and sails into the high heavens, the service begins. The courtyards in millions of small, poor homes are changed to fairyland because the goddess touches them with her silver fingers. She hides the poverty and ugliness of everyday things; she smooths away the wrinkles from tired faces, and lends a grace to awkward silhouettes as they approach her table. One after another the women go forward and make their vows. Two candles are lighted because it is customary to offer them in pairs. Bundles of incense sticks are stuck flaming in the family urn; their light glimmers but faintly in the flood of moonshine. The whole service lasts but a few moments and concludes with the attaching of a poster to the wall of the house, showing the moon rabbit under the sacred cassia tree, pounding the pill of immortality in his mortar. Ceremonious salutations are addressed to this quaint little animal figure. Then his picture is taken down and burned. Thus ends the religious rites proper to the Eighth Moon Festival.

Kite Day in China

In many places in China the ninth day of the ninth moon is given over to kiteflying. Thousands gather on the surrounding hills, and special police are often sent out to keep order because rivalry among the kitefliers sometimes leads to clan fights. The

117

festival kites are huge affairs. They require four or five grown men to manipulate them, men with the strong arm yet light wrist of an expert fencer. Chinese gentlemen of leisure, averse to more violent sports, form societies and purchase a monster kite to take to the air in competition with their neighbors.

On Kite Day the sky is populated with dragons, butterflies, centipedes, and cunningly devised figures which by means of simple mechanisms worked by the wind roll their eyes, move their paws, and flutter their wings. The battle in the sky is accompanied by eerie sounds—shrieks and moans from the tiny Aeolian harps attached to each competitor's kite. Some enthusiasts wait until dark, attach lanterns to their kites, and fly them again. This time, the flying creatures curtsey and bow to one another in greeting until they are devoured by the night.

HARVEST FESTIVALS

Harvest festivals come at a time of year when the last warmth of Indian summer has gone, and bleak winds and gray skies begin to appear. It is the time of year when barns are made snug, the last of the fruit and vegetables are stored away in bins, and people sit in front of a roaring fire to relax from their long summer's work. In short, it is a rejoicing over earth's gifts.

The custom of holding a festival at harvesttime goes back two thousand years. Beautiful harvest festivals are celebrated in every nation, each in it's own way. In the United States it is called "Thanksgiving." The Irish build tremendous bonfires to offer encouragement to the waning sun; the Jews call their harvest festival *Sukkot*, which commemorates their yearly pilgrimage to Jerusalem to offer their thanksgiving as directed in the Bible.

> Three times a year shalt all thy males appear before the Lord thy God in the place where He shall choose; on the Feast of the Unleavened Bread, on the Feast of Weeks, and on the Feast of Tabernacles; and they shall not appear before the Lord empty; every male shall give as he is able, according to the blessing of the Lord thy God which He has given thee.

118

Many harvest festivals have preserved their gay and joyous spirit to this day, but their agricultural and religious significances are often obscure. Because the nights grew longer, many festivals serve the triple purpose of bidding goodbye to summer, welcoming winter, and remembering the dead. Most common of all customs is for children to dress up in costumes, wear masks, and go begging from door to door.

ALL HALLOW'S EVE—HALLOWEEN—OCTOBER 31

Girls and boys in many lands look forward to Halloween, October 31, as the most exciting festival of the year. The eve of any festival is supposed to be a solemn vigil, but two festival eves have lost nearly all trace of such serious tones. One, of course, is Halloween, the eve of All Saints' Day, and the other is Christmas Eve.

All over Canada and the United States children dress as ragamuffins, ghosts, elves, and farmers, and go from house to house carrying paper bags for handouts. The most fun is to wear masks so they can play tricks on their neighbors.

Many Halloween customs come from Ireland and Great Britain, such as tossing objects into a fire—stones, vegetables, and nuts —to keep the spooks away. Country folk hollowed out turnips and pumpkins and place a lighted candle inside to scare evil spirits away from the house. It was also the custom for English children to dress up in one another's clothing (boys donning girl's outfits and vice versa) and to wear masks to go begging from door to door for "soul cakes."

It was the Irish who initiated the "trick or treat" system hundreds of year ago. Groups of Irish farmers would go from house to house soliciting food for the village. Prosperity was promised to cheerful givers and threats were made against tightfisted donors.

For the past fifteen years in the United States, and more recently in other countries, millions of boys and girls have found a different way to celebrate "trick or treat." Instead of collecting goodies for themselves, they say, "Trick or treat for UNICEF."

119

The pennies, nickels, and dimes they collect are used by the United Nations to help sick and hungry children around the world.

After trick-or-treating, groups of children get together for a well-earned Halloween party. First they empty their orange-and-black UNICEF cartons into a huge caldron. Then there are prizes for the best costumes, fortune-telling games, bobbing for apples, and lots of candy, cake, and ice cream.

ENGLAND, GUY FAWKES DAY—NOVEMBER 5

Guy Fawkes Day has many customs in common with a Halloween celebration in the United States. The holiday arose out of a religious conflict when Roman Catholic priests were banished from England: several Catholic Englishmen organized a plot to blow up the House of Parliament in the name of religious freedom. They hid thirty-six barrels of gunpowder in the vaults of the buildings. On November 5, 1605, the plot was discovered and the conspirators tried and executed. Guy Fawkes is the individual most remembered because he had been chosen to set off the explosion.

Today Guy Fawkes Day is mainly a holiday for children, who observe it by dressing up in funny costumes, having parades, lighting firecrackers, and making straw dummies of Guy Fawkes. Sometimes he is propped up on a cart or on the sidewalk while children who are his guardians beg "a penny for the Guy" from passers-by. In some towns, Guy dummies are burned in bonfires.

Since the Gunpowder Plot of 1605, it has been a tradition on every Guy Fawkes Day for the Royal Yeomen of the Guard, dressed in their traditional "beefeater" costumes, to prowl through the vaults beneath the Houses of Parliament in a mock search for the explosives.

AUSTRIA, WINE FESTIVAL ON ST. MARTIN'S DAY, NOVEMBER 11

The opening of the new-wine season is usually celebrated on St. Martin's Day, November 11, and the new wine is sampled in a festive manner to the accompaniment of a delicious, crisp-roasted "Martin's" goose, stewed in wine. The Hueriger Parties at Grunzig, Sievering, and Nussdorf—all suburbs of Vienna—are the most popular wine celebrations, but many more cities where wine is made also hold them.

These feasts of new wine and old song have a great tradition, dating back to the era of St. Joseph II, son of Maria Theresa, who encouraged his people in this form of jollity in order to keep them from too much concern about what he was doing in the political field.

At the three places named, small bushes are hung outside the door to indicate that the establishment is open to customers. It is the custom to take one's own picnic meal, although one can usually buy a snack on the spot. But the main thing is the wine and congenial companionship.

ST. MARTIN FESTIVAL IN GERMANY

In Germany, Martinsfest is a double festival honoring St. Martin and Martin Luther. St. Martin, the fourth century friend of children and the poor, is especially revered along the Lower Rhine. One of the most picturesque festivals takes place in Düsseldorf, where huge torchlight processions of children go through the streets. Many of the participants carry hollowed-out pumpkin lanterns, illuminated from within with lighted candles. St. Martin, followed by hundreds of children, rides through the street represented by a person in costume. Just as German Catholic communities honor St. Martin, Protestant groups celebrate Martin

Luther's birthday with picturesque rites. In Erfurt, where Martin Luther attended the University, thousands of children with lighted lanterns form a procession which finally marches up the Plaza in front of the cathedral of the Severi Church. There the children form with their lanterns the "Luther Rose."

CEREMONIES IN AFRICA

Those who hope to see war dances in Africa usually go away disappointed. Most performances lack ceremonial significance, as the problems of an African have to do with life itself—food, shelter, birth, death. Food is most important and the quantity depends on the luck of the hunter who goes to the river for fish or into the forests for game. In parts of Uganda, for instance, at certain seasons of the year tribesmen gather in groups for a ceremony to capture wild game.

Blessing of the Spears

In isolated Karamija District of Uganda, 175,000 pastoral herdsmen dwell all but untouched by civilization. Napore spearsmen perform a ceremony before each hunt to placate the evil spirits and to implore the sun to bring them luck. The spears are blessed by the old men of the tribe, too old to hunt, then the hunters fan out through the bush to look for antelopes.

Fisherman's Prayer

The Fanti men—roving fishermen along the Atlantic shore—to the accompaniment of drums raise their voices in prayer:

"Oh, fish spirit, lead the fishes to the nets. Lead only the big ones, let the little ones go away unharmed, make the nets strong so they will hold the fishes."

SUKKOT—JEWISH HARVEST FESTIVAL

Sukkot commemorates the occasion when pilgrims from all parts of Judea journeyed to the central shrine on Mount Zion with offerings from their harvest. *Sukkah* (sometimes spelled *suka*) means "hut," the temporary abode of those who lived in the fields during the harvest season. Observant Jews to this day build a sukkah, outdoors if possible or in the synagogue proper. This is made of scraps from field and forest and decorated with produce from the harvest. Much art and poetry have been inspired by the family gatherings in colorful sukkahs. Every Jew is enjoined to visit the sukkah with his loved ones and friends and have at least one meal in it.

Rabbinic laws specify the sukkah's construction. It must symbolize the brevity and insecurity of human life. It must not be built of solid masonry; the roof must allow the stars to be seen and the rain to come through, reminding man of God beyond.

In time the festival acquired a historical significance and came to symbolize the tents in which the Isrealites dwelt in the wilderness on their way to the Promised Land. This is part of the historic tendency in Judaism to emphasize memory of Egyptian servitude, but Sukkot retains more of the agricultural significance, with all the color of joy and harvest.

GREECE, ST. MENAS' DAY—NOVEMBER 11

Mênas means the Messenger, the Revealer; to send word, to instruct. It is therefore believed that this saint has the power to reveal where stolen or lost articles lie hidden. His name is particularly invoked by shepherds who have lost their sheep, or who wish to protect their flocks against wolves. St. Mênas' Day is for the shepherds. Shepherd's wives refrain from using scissors on this day; indeed, they wind a thread around the scissors' mouth, a symbolic action meant to keep the wolves' jaws closed. It is also intended to keep the village gossips' mouths shut.

On St. Mênas' Day or thereabouts the first chilly message of winter makes itself felt. There is a popular proverb which says: "I [winter] send word of my coming on St. Mênas Day and I arrive on St. Philip's [November 15]."

UNITED STATES, THANKSGIVING

In the United States, Thanksgiving is more of a "feast day" than any other holiday on the calendar. It is celebrated on the last Thursday in November according to Proclamation by the president. Traditionally it celebrates the first abundant harvest of the Pilgrim fathers who originally settled on the New England shores. It comes at the time of year when New England country folk used to slaughter animals and salt them down for the year; the cellars were full of apples and late vegetables (pumpkins, turnips, parsnips, carrots), and turkeys and geese were in their prime. Also, to most people, Thanksgiving dinner marked the last big meal of the season. Everyone knew full well that winter was fast approaching and food would not be plentiful and would be lacking in variety.

Thanksgiving is, almost without exception, the family's day. Thanksgiving dinners are family affairs and celebrated almost entirely within the home. Many people celebrate Thanksgiving by attending a church service in the morning, and in many localities persons of different faiths worship together. It is also a time for sharing with the less fortunate, and churches, schools, and many philanthropic societies see to it that no one goes hungry. To many, it is the one day in the year they remember to give thanks for all America has done for them.

VIRGIN ISLANDS, HURRICANE THANKSGIVING

The people of the Virgin Islands have two Thanksgivings. They celebrate one on the day set aside in the United States, but there is also a Thanksgiving Day on October 25. At this time the Islanders give thanks if there have been no hurricanes for a year. There is also a "love feast" that follows the Hurricane Thanksgiving, celebrated by the parishioners of the Moravian Church. Following the services, the people feast on buns filled with raisins and drink a bright red beverage made of raspberries.

THANKSGIVING FOR BIRDS—AMERICAN INDIANS

It was an "olde" Indian custom to hang three ears of corn and a gourd outside the teepee for the birds. After a plentiful harvest in the fall, the Indians thanked their God for permitting them proper weather and endurance for the crop they would yield for the three forthcoming seasons—fall, winter, and spring. Then it was customary to hang the corn facing the west. The gourd, representing the fourth season, was placed or hung toward the south, meaning that the gourd, being hollow and dry, with a few morsels of seed inside, needed the sun of summer, and by the time of the fourth season, the gourd or seeds would be all they would have left. When the birds came to peck at the corn, they were representing Him from the heavens accepting His gift.

The Indians had a similar custom when planting corn: they placed four kernels in each mound along with a fish. The Pilgrims, being English and rather thrifty, made up a well-known nursery rhyme:

> One for the Blackbird
> Two for the crow
> Three for the cutworm
> And four to grow!

Another Indian custom was to place a pumpkin, outside, which was hollowed out and lit to ward off the "hobgobblins" or *Wiem-woo* ("frost"). Much like the smudge pots of today, they would burn fat inside them to protect their harvest if there was an early frost.

11. ADVENT

Make ready for the way of the Lord. MATTHEW 3:3

The sacred season called Advent (Coming) became widely observed in the ninth century and still is in Christian homes and churches. It begins on Sunday nearest the feast of St. Andrew (November 30) and embraces the following four weeks, including Christmas Eve. While no special feast is prescribed, prayers and liturgical services stress preparation for the Lord's Nativity.

Advent traditions vary from place to place, but always the four-week period is looked upon as a happy time as people prepare for the greatest Christian festival of the year. Many beautiful customs are practiced in the home as well as in the church. Daily, at a certain time (usually in the evening), the whole family may gather for a religious exercise and a moment of peace and contemplation. These ceremonies have lasting impressions on the minds of children, remembering their love for the "day upon which a Savior was born to mankind."

STAR OF SEVEN

Many German households have a "Star of Seven," which is a seven-branched candlestick. The candles are lighted on each Sunday in Advent—one on the first, two on the second, three on the third, and so on. Members of the family or groups of friends sit about the lighted tapers singing seasonal carols and preparing handmade gifts for Christmas.

TWO EUROPEAN CHRISTMAS MARKETS

Marseille, France, Santon Fair

The Santon Fair takes place throughout December in Marseille, France. "Santons" are the little colored clay figures with which the Christmas *créches* are peopled, and thousands come from far around to the Fair to purchase them. Over the years a multitude of purely local figures, dressed in costumes of old Provence, have been added to the ones of biblical narratives. These gaily colored clay statues (the clay is not baked) have a naïve grace. They are

128

the work of a score of local families; molds and models have been handed down from father to son since the seventeenth century.

Christmas Market in Nuremberg

The principal reasons for the Nuremburg market's fame are that only things directly connected with Christmas are permitted to be offered for sale, and the entire structure of the festival is based on artistic good taste. As a result, it is attended by visitors from many countries. The main market square is the excellent setting, in view of the famous *Schöner Brunnen* ("Beautiful Fountain") and the 600-year-old *Franenkirche*—"Our Lady's church."

The festival lasts three weeks, from early December until Christmas, and the mayor and town council take part in the opening ceremonies. The mart is inaugurated by choral singing and trumpet melodies from the church gallery, where a child dressed as the Christ child and two gold-leaf-angels pronounce a rhymed invitation to visit Kris Kringle's mart. The ringing of church bells, the singing of Christmas carols, fairylike illuminations, artistic decorations, and some ten thousand children are a part of the spectacle. The entire mart centers on a large Christmas crib in the market square, Medieval lanterns, artistic signs, sheds, pavilions, and booths—all in uniform Christmas style—and last but not least, the scent of such goodies as fried sausages.

Shortly before Christmas, a candlelight procession of Nuremberg children carrying homemade lanterns moves through the city. Daily round trips by romantically decorated horse-drawn coaches are made. This festival has a history of more than four hundred years, and in the sixteenth and seventeenth centuries foreign royalties and their suites came to admire and enjoy this unique event.

ST. NICHOLAS DAY—DECEMBER 6

In Northern European Countries

The role of St. Nicholas in northern Europe is that of a heavenly messenger coming at the beginning of Advent. It is on this feast day that the children's Christmas festival really begins. St. Nicholas is represented as a tall, venerable, kind-faced man, wearing the cape of a bishop with the miter headdress. With him one finds the dark-skinned companion known as Black Peter, who always carries a bunch of switches. He promises sweets to those who are good and threatens punishment to boys and girls who are bad, unless they mend their naughty ways.

St. Nicholas rides a white horse followed by a cart laden with parcels to be left at different houses. Before they go to sleep, children stuff their shoes with hay and place them on the window sill so the horse will have something to eat during the journey.

Of course, St. Nicholas always replaces the hay with candy and small gfits while Black Peter distributes switches to parents of children who are bad.

St. Nicholas Day in Greece

St. Nicholas Day takes place at a time when winter cold becomes sharper, as confirmed by the popular saying, "Here comes St. Nicholas, loaded with snow." This is the time when storms begin to happen. Perhaps it is for this reason St. Nicholas has come to be worshipped as the patron saint of seamen. According to popular tradition, his clothes are always drenched with brine, his beard drips with sea water, and his brow is covered with perspiration due to his continual efforts to reach sinking ships in time to save them from the angry waves.

St. Nicholas is lord of the tempest. No Greek ship, no matter how small, travels without his icon on board. Seamen always take a disk of *kollyva* ("boiled wheat grain"), blessed during the service of St. Nicholas, before they put out to sea. If the ship meets with a rough sea, they throw the *killyva* into the waters, saying, "Dear St. Nicholas, cease your rush." It is believed that as soon as St. Nicholas' *kollyva* touches the water, or better still, if his icon is plunged in as well, the wind will cease. When a ship is in danger of perishing at sea, the skipper promises to bring St. Nicholas a silver or gold ex-voto, representing his ship, if he reaches land safely. The skipper and sailors carry this offering to the church barefooted; a service is held, and the offering is hung on the icon of the Saint.

FEAST OF IMMACULATE CONCEPTION— DECEMBER 8

Philippine Islands, A Ride for Our Lady

One of the many, varied ways in which Filipinos celebrate feast days of their patron saints is by having a river parade. This is not strange to anyone who has any acquaintance at all with the topography of the Philippines; almost anywhere one turns there is the blue sea or a part of a long river or a green lake to meet the eye.

In the little fishing village of Malabon, in central Luzon, the citizens render homage and thanksgiving to its patroness, Our Lady of Immaculate Conception, by a yearly river procession up and down the Navotas River.

Nine days before the eighth of December, the people start offering a novena of prayers and Masses in the parish church. On the night of the eighth, the image of Our Lady is enthroned on a beautifully decorated, brightly lit stand, which is then shouldered by husky men and carried in procession to the wharf. Amid noise, singing, and band music, the image is lifted up to a richly decorated motorboat in which are waiting as many people as can be accommodated.

Music for Our Lady

Old women then begin to sing and dance around the statue, their wrinkled brows graced with strings of *sampaguita*, the national flower. Young women and children sing the *Immaculate Mother* alternately with the band. The people would never let their Lady and Mother go alone. Every available banca in the

131

town is out to form a convoy around the Queen's vessel, gaily inching its way three or four times up and down the river.

A feature very special to the river procession at Malabon occurs the third time around, when the vessel docks on the other side of the river where the statue of St. Joseph, carried by the people of the other parish, await Our Lady. There the two images are carried in procession to the parish church of St. Joseph. The *Salve Regina* is sung and the two are returned to the wharf. Our Lady is again raised up on her dais, and the whole fleet of bancas noisily roar back to the home church, where she is returned to her place of honor.

People come from many places to join in this touching devotion. The procession is made to show deep gratitude to Our Lady for the good catch of fish the people have had the previous year and to ask for her continued help in the future.

DAY OF STE LUCIA—DECEMBER 13

Sweden

On December 13, which is the darkest day of the winter in Sweden, the oldest daughter of the house, dressed in sparkling white, plays Ste Lucia, queen of lights. She serves to remind everyone that soon in this northern country the days will be longer and spring will be on its way.

Lucia wears a beautiful red sash about her waist, and on her head is an astonishing crown of pine boughs haloed with the light of seven candles. Early in the morning, accompanied by her brothers and sisters, she goes to her parents' room, awakening them with the song "Santa Lucia."

The next oldest daughter has tinsel in her hair and wears a white robe. She carries a candle in her hand, as do all the other children. The oldest son, "the star boy," is dressed in a white robe and high-pointed cap decked with silver stars.

Lucia carries a large tray of coffee and buns, the buns usually a special holiday treat called "Lucia's Cats." They are made of strips of saffron dough and raisin eyes. The family gather around the tray while Lucia pours each a cup of coffee and passes the cakes, proclaiming the arrival of the Christmas season.

Italy

In Syracuse, Italy, said to be the birthplace of Ste Lucia, two important *festas* are held in the saint's honor. One is celebrated on December 13, date of her birth, the other somewhat later.

On December 5 her silver image and *bier*, kept under lock and key in the cathedral, are taken to her church in the Bargo of Santa Lucia. There they remain exposed until the eve of the thirteenth, when they are returned in a magnificent procession to the cathedral, through iluminated streets between houses decorated with rich colorful cloths. The heavy silver *bier* is borne on the shoulders of strong men who vie with each other for the honor, and members of the carpenter fraternity, wearing black frocks compete for the right to ring a little silver bell to mark the pauses.

The second *festa* for Santa Lucia commemorates a miracle. Once when the city was suffering from famine and the church and the city had exhausted all their resources, a ship laden with corn sailed into port. Its arrival was announced by a dove flying into the cathedral where the people were praying to Santa Lucia. During this *festa*, the *bier* is taken to the church near the cathedral and is returned in a procession under a shower of flowers and with a dove flying overhead.

133

Hanukkah is a joyous festival celebrating the first great victory for religious freedom won by the Jews more than two thousand years ago. It is celebrated for eight days, beginning the twenty-fifth of the Hebrew month Kislev (November–December). When Judas Maccabee's men were cleaning the temple, they found a single jar of holy oil, only enough to keep the Holy Light before the Holy Ark burning for one day. Miraculously, this one jar burned for eight days and nights. For this reason Maccabee proclaimed an eight-day holiday to celebrate the rededication to God.

Today children love this holiday, not only because it has become a time for giving of small gifts—very often distributed on each of the eight nights—but also because Hanukkah is the traditional time for playing the dreidel game.

The big event of Hanukkah is the candlelighting ceremony commemorating the light that burned for eight days during the redemption of the temple. Every night of the festival, the father of the family places candles in a special candelabrum called the menorah. In the presence of the whole family, he lights one candle the first night, two the second night, and so on, until all eight candles are lit on the last night, always using a helper candle called the *shamos* to carry the flame.

In the city of Tel Aviv—called the "City of Light" at Hanukkah because all the lights in the city are left on during the festival—every public building displays its own menorah, illuminating an additional candle each night as one does in the home.

12. CHRISTMAS THE WORLD OVER

In all the year, there is no day that fills the heart of the world with so much joy as Christmas. Since the most ancient times, people of all races have held festivals or feast days on which they ate, drank, and made merry—generally in honor of their gods. Christmas is the most important festival in Christian countries, celebrating the birth of Jesus, and people all over the world express their joy and devotion in their own individual ways. The celebration begins with Advent (first Sunday in December) and continues on to Twelfth Night (January 6). In many lands, the Christmas festival is interwoven with ancient folklore and legends that have been handed down for generations to the present day. This is especially true in Africa and Asia where the Christmas story is comparatively new, having been introduced during the past century by Christian missionaries.

THE GIVING OF GIFTS

It has been the practice of people throughout the ages to set aside a certain period of the year in which, through the giving of gifts, they may share the good things of life with each other. In

Christian countries, Christmas became the season for exchanging presents. There are many forms of making gifts, particularly to children. In Scandinavia, gifts are left by little gnomelike creatures that live in the attic all through the year; St. Nicholas and his companion Peter bring gifts on December 6 to children in northern European countries, and the Bonhomme Noël leaves presents for French children on the hearth; two women, Babushka in the Soviet Union and Befana in Italy, both depicted as being old and wrinkled, are the bearers of gifts. Gift-giving in the Middle East is closely associated with the Nativity, with the Three Wise Men arriving by camels with gifts for the children.

In the United States, New York has had through the years a close association with Christmas gift-giving. Early Dutch settlers, for instance, introduced St. Nicholas to America. On West Twenty-third Street, Clement Clark Moore wrote "A Visit From St. Nicholas," and on the same street lived Thomas Nast, the famed cartoonist who gave Santa the red suit, whiskers, and pot belly by which we recognize him today. Washington Irving lived at Seventeenth Street and Irving Place and he wrote such short stories as "Christmas at Brackenbridge Hall," "Christmas Dinners," and "Christmas." O. Henry was living just around the corner from Irving's house when he wrote the "Gift of the Magi"; Charles Dickens read his "A Christmas Carol" in Steinway Hall on East Fourteenth Street; and from a house in the West Nineties, eight-year-old Virginia O'Hanlon wrote to the New York Sun asking if there really was a Santa Claus. "Yes, Virginia," the editor began his classic reply, "there is a Santa Claus."

Because people travel and communicate with all parts of the world, it is not necessary to enlarge on the customs, the meaning of the festival, and the happenings connected with the celebration of Christmas. The holiday has become so universal as to be almost the same in all Western lands. However, each individual country usually has one or two distinctive features that are still practiced in this modern age. Here are a number of them from all parts of the world that can be adapted to modern Christmas pageants,

136

church and school programs, community celebrations, or parties
in the home.

In the United States every parish church has a special service
on Christmas morning that includes carols and retelling of the
Christmas Story. During the week there are other types of programs—a "Service by Candlelight" on Christmas Eve, cantatas,
and a party or dramatic production for young people in the community. In Catholic churches a solemn service of Vespers is held
directly before the Midnight Mass. During the service, bells ring
out through the winter night to announce the coming of the
Saviour.

America is inhabited by people from all sections of Europe and
Asia, and Christmas comes to each of them in their different traditions. To start on the Atlantic seaboard, in New England villages
bands of carolers, ringing hand bells, lift up their voices on
Christmas Eve. In Philadelphia are descendants of Swedish settlers, and the legend of Ste Lucia, with her candlelighted wreath
of leaves, is recalled. In other parts the state the Pennsylvania
Dutch construct elaborate Putz (the Christmas crib), including
a whole landscape of sheep, camels, and buildings, as well as a
tree. In the South, where the day is warm, the night sky is filled
with fireworks. California boasts of having the most elaborate
Christmas festival, which is staged in a most spectacular location
—the Yosemite National Park. At dusk men dressed in white-caped
and cowled costumes, to represent ancient Druids, gather from all
directions and enter an age-old hotel, chanting melodies and
bearing an enormous yule log. The log is placed ceremoniously
in the great fireplace and lighted with a brand that has been
treasured from the log of the year before.

In states that border on Mexico, one hears the *Posada* sung, in
which people in the towns enact the story of the search for lodging for Mary and Joseph. Thus, Christmas in America has many
moods.

Northern Countries

Because of their location, Scandinavia and countries bordering on the Baltic Sea have incorporated many traditions from the ancient Yule festival of northern Europe. These have to do with celebrating the lengthening of the day and the return of the sun rites practiced by the Druids. Also many people consider the season as a period when the spirits of the dead return. Many Christmas customs are preparations for receiving these guests; the house is cleaned and special food prepared for the return of the loved ones on Christmas Day.

Church Service

Faithful to age-old custom people delight, whenever possible, to drive to church in a sleigh for an early morning Christmas service. Since the night is still black, the church-goers in some parts of the northern European countries light their way through a snowy, silent forest with flaring torches.

Yule Men

These are little spritelike men depicted as having long white beards and wearing red toboggans or caps. They are representative of many supernatural beings who in old days played a part in the Yue festival. Each country has its own endearing Christmas personality such as Julenisse in Norway, Jultomten in Sweden, and

Nisse in Denmark.

The Yule men are given to all sorts of mischief but are good little gnomes. For one thing, they keep a friendy eye on cows and horses in the barn. No one ever actually sees them but they appear occasionally in strings of colorful paper cutouts and on post cards. Children are wont to place a platter of rice porridge outside the kitchen door for them on Christmas Eve, and of course, by morning it has disappeared.

Finland has a strange Yule man they call "Joukupukki." He is a small creature dressed in the costume of a goat. A set of handsome horns is mounted on his head and his hands and feet are covered with the skin and hoofs of a goat.

Christmas Decorations

In many cities and small towns, display windows have a green frame of fir garlands. Garlands are also stretched from lamppost to lamppost in the streets, decorated at suitable intervals with papier-mâché Christmas bells and stars interspersed with myriads of electric lights when dusk comes on. Since the northern European countries are predominately Lutheran, the little white church made of plaster and placed on a slab of cotton (to give an allusion of snow), with red lights showing through gothic windows, is included in all decorations. Storekeepers conjure up enormous snowscapes with everything from picturesque windmills to commemorative flags and colors. Invariably the little electric train, when it runs a certain distance, must disappear into a tunnel and then re-appear again.

Christmas Trees

Since this is Hans Christian Andersen's part of the world, the tree is a guest in almost every home. In his tale "The Fir Tree," he tells how the tree is picked in the woods and brought into the house where it is decorated with little nets and pine cones and hearts cut out of colored paper, with sweets and gilded apples and nuts hanging from its branches. "Was I really born to such glorious destiny?" the fir tree wondered.

Christmas Cookies

The making of cookies is a household art in northern Europe, especially during the Christmas season. They are used not only as a sweet but for gifts to friends and for tree decorations. The cookies are rolled and cut into many different shapes and may be divided into two classes: one a light sugar-cookie and the other made of a dark dough containing dark molasses. They are cut into traditional shapes according to their color: brown cookies into shapes of men, birds, dogs, sheep, roosters, and other animals; light cookies into semblances of stars, angels, hearts, trees, and flowers.

Food for Birds and Animals

One of the most charming customs in northern countries is the remembrance of animals and birds at Christmas, since they were present at the birth of the Holy babe. The farm beasts are carefully tended, and the cattle are given extra fodder. But the most beautiful of all customs is saved for the birds. An especially gleaned sheath, saved from the fall harvest, is placed on top of a tall pole in the yard, and on Christmas morning every gable, gateway, and barn door is decorated with a bundle of grain, the birds' Christmas dinner.

Christmas Customs

Here are some delightful Christmas customs indigenous to northern European countries.

Norway. During the German occupation of Norway, every year one of Norway's M.T.B. boats stationed in England was dispatched to bring back a Norway spruce to be presented as a gift to King Haakon, who spent the war years in England. This practice of bringing a Norwegian tree to England was continued after the war and each Christmas a huge Norwegian spruce stands in London's Trafalgar Square, a gift from the Norwegian people.

Sweden. It has become the custom of holding Lucia beauty contents on Ste Lucia's Day, December 13, in city offices and clubs. Of course, the prettiest girl is Lucia. Usually there is a party, and cakes called *Lussekatter*, or "Lucia cats" are served. They symbolize good luck, since the cat is supposed to keep the devil away.

Holland. In Holland, before Christmas Day arrives, all presents intended for the *Julklapp* delivery must be prepared by enclosing them in a great many wrappings of various kinds. None should suggest the contents in any way. The following description is typical of the time and effort this custom consumes.

If one of the presents is a trinket, wrap it up in fringed paper such as is used for candy or sugar kisses, place it in a small box, tie the box with a narrow ribbon. Then do it up in common brown paper and wrap the package with strips of cloth until it is round like a ball. Cover this with a layer of dough and brown in the oven. Finally, pin it up in a napkin, wrap it in white wrapping paper, and tie with a pink string.

Denmark publishes a Christmas stamp each year. Because the stamp is used in the cause of charity, the Danes overstamp letters in countries all over the world. The Christmas stamp was invented in 1904 by a Danish postmaster, and nowadays people in Denmark would not dare post a Christmas card without making it unrecognizable by sticking stamps everywhere.

Germany. The Advent wreath, an old Christian custom, originated with the Lutherans in Germany. It is simply a circle of greenery around which four candles, one for each week of Advent, are equally spaced. One candle is lighted the first Sunday in Advent and an additional one each week thereafter, until on Christmas Eve the wreath is a glowing testament of the nearness of the Saviour. Each Sunday, upon lighting the candle, the family join in saying a short prayer, or in reading a verse from the Scriptures. Often friends are invited to join the family circle, to take part in the exercise and to sing Christmas carols.

Belgium. One requirement for all Nativity plays in Flanders is that each character who participates must resemble some figure from one of Brueghel's paintings. This limits the use of costumes to those that were worn by ordinary people in the sixteenth century.

141

Countries under the domination of the Soviet Union still observe a few traditional Christmas customs, particularly religious ones celebrated by the Orthodox Church.

Russia. Since the Revolution little of the old traditional Christmas customs remain. On Christmas Eve it is customary to fast until after the first service of the church, which means generally the Eastern Orthodox, though there are other smaller religious groups. Frequently the ceremony of blessing the house and household is observed. Priests visit the homes, accompanied by boys carrying vessels of holy water, and sprinkle a little in each room. Christmas trees are common but more recently have been called New Year trees. A brightly lighted revolving tree, sometimes seventy-five feet tall, stands in St. George's Hall in the Grand Kremlin Palace.

Romania. In Romania, boys go from house to house singing carols, reciting poetry and legends during the Christmas season. The leader of the group carries a large wooden star called a *Steaua*, which is covered with gilt paper and adorned with bells and frills of colored ribbons. A picture of the Holy Family is painted or pasted in the center, which is illuminated with a candle, and the whole is attached to a stout pole such as the handle of a broomstick.

Poland. In Poland, Christmas dinner is served just as the evening star appears in the winter sky. The meal consists of twelve courses—one for each Apostle. They have a saying, "Our hearts are open to a stranger, kith or kin"; so one empty seat is always left at the table in case an unknown traveler should appear to share the meal.

Switzerland

In many Swiss villages, children celebrate *Sternsineen,* or "Star Singing," with an elaborate pageant. Three are chosen to dress as kings. They march in a torchlight procession, bearing gifts to the manger scene, where others portray members of the Holy Family. Around the manger stand "angels" wearing white robes and halos, holding a great illuminated "Star of Bethlehem" on a tall pole.

These countries, France, Portugal, Spain, and Italy, being predominantly Catholic, have Christmas customs that are tied to the Church. The season is a joyous celebration of the Nativity, not only in the houses of God but also in the homes of the people. The church is decorated with garlands of green and beautiful flowers as at no other time of year. Altars are shiny white and silver dotted with yellow flames from dozens of small white candles. Priests dressed in white and gold, assisted by acolytes, carry lighted tapers and pots of incense.

THE THREE MASSES

From early times the Three Masses have survived as the very heart of the Christmas festival. They signify the mystical drama of the coming of the Saviour:

The Missa in Nocte ("during the night") to signify the Eternal Birth of the Word of God in the Father.

The Missa in Aurora ("at dawn") to signify the Birth of the Son of God in the flesh, or the Temporal Birth.

The Missa in Die ("during the day") to signify the Birth of Christ in the hearts of the faithful, the Spiritual Birth.

Midnight has never been assigned as the official time for the first Mass, it is merely prescribed that it be said during the night. In some churches it is celebrated before dawn at four or five in the morning; and in early centuries, it was celebrated about three o'clock, "when the cock crows."

CHRISTMAS CRIB

In every Catholic church the world over the Christmas crib is unveiled just before midnight. The drama reinforces the people's love for the Saviour, and the groundwork is laid for a joyous celebration of the Nativity. The service is celebrated in varying ways, depending on the country.

In Alaska, Eskimos come into the missions from frozen wilder-

nesses to see the unveiling of the Nativity. Philippine churches keep their crib amid a blaze of pink, green, blue, and white candles all during the Christmas season. In India, it is surrounded by tropical ferns, red, pink, and blue flowers, colored streamers, and rich tapestries. The crib in Africa and parts of Asia may be made of rough brick against a backdrop of brush, or the American Indian of the plains may make his of straw with a snow-covered roof. Each one, no matter how elaborate, calls to mind the essential meaning of the feast.

In Catholic homes everywhere the Christmas crib is constructed with loving care as a part of the decoration or center of special Christmas ceremonies. Since the time of St. Francis, farmers in mountain areas of Central Europe have spent the long winter evenings of Advent repairing and enlarging their beautiful cribs. The scene is sometimes made up of hundreds of figures that have been handed down from generation to generation. There are many versions of the mystic drama, but always there is the central group —the Christ child in His cradle, Mary and Joseph, and people and animals about Him.

Associated with Midnight Mass is the informal *réveillon*, a late meal that follows soon afterward in the home. It combines reunion and thanksgiving as well as refreshments. In some homes, the figure of the Christ child is solemnly placed in the crib while the family gather around to sing Christmas carols. Sometimes a Yule log is lit and the father conducts a ceremony to ask a blessing on the house.

CHRISTMAS CELEBRATIONS

France. Père Noël brings gifts to French children along with a companion named Père Fouettard, who is stern and full of discipline. He reminds Père Noël exactly how each child has behaved during the past year. In some parts of France, St. Nicholas Day, December 6, is the beginning of Christmas and Père Noël visits the home on St. Nicholas Eve and puts gifts in children's shoes. Then, the children expect another visit from the gift-giver on December 25. In some places it is from Père Noël and in others the gifts are thought to come directly from *le petit Jésus.*

After Midnight Mass the French usually hold family parties in which a late supper is served. At this meal, goose is served in many parts of the country. It is said that the reason for serving a goose dinner is because geese welcomed the Wise Men as they approached the stable where the Christ child lay.

It is pleasing to know that in some parts of France the little wren is looked upon with much affection. It is called *Poulette de Dieu* because the wren is supposed to have brought soft feathers and moss to make the little blanket for the Christ child.

Spain. Christmas is a thoroughly religious day in Spain. During part of the day, service people visit patron after patron to leave cards or small verses and greetings. To each door come the carpenters, the delivery boys, the bakers, the shoemakers, and others associated with service to the community. It is, of course, an indication of their wish to serve again during the coming year. They are given modest presents in the spirit of the day, usually money.

Spanish children expect their gifts at Epiphany, January 6, which commemorates the coming of the Three Wise Men to Bethlehem, bearing gifts to the Christ child. The children leave their shoes on the window sills or balconies and they fill them with straw and carrots or barley (*cebada*) for the horses of the Magi. Their favorite Wise Man is Balthazar, who rides a donkey. He brings the gifts and always includes a bit of sweet candy called *turrón*.

Italy. On Epiphany Eve, Befana goes around giving presents to children. Italian people say her work is to go forth for ever and ever on Epiphany to search for the Christ child.

According to legend, Befana lived in a cottage by a highway where a caravan made up of men dressed as kings and riding camels stopped to inquire the way to Bethlehem. They told her they were in search of a *bambino* who was born to be king. They asked her to accompany them but she refused because she had just lost her husband and child to the plague and did not want to leave.

The next day a shepherd told her who the visitors were, and she decided to go to see the *bambino* and give it some of the things her own baby wore. She started out but could not find the caravan and did not know where Bethlehem was, so for two thousand years she has wandered, trying to find the Three Wise Men. She is depicted as being old and wrinkled but with goodness showing from her eyes.

On each morning throughout the Christmas season most Italian families pray before the Presepio and light candles. The Presepio, symbolic of a Christmas tree, is found in every Italian home. It is made with a framework of lathlike strips of wood with three or four shelves, graduating in size from top to bottom. Usually it is painted in several colors and decorated with tufts and tassels and greens. The upper shelves are used to hold gifts, and some are laden with candy and nuts. On the bottom shelf is placed the infant Jesus, surrounded by shepherds, saints, and angels.

Greece. Christmas is not as important in Greece as it is in the West. It is chiefly a religious festival, but a number of popular customs are observed.

On Christmas Eve, the village children pour out into the streets and go from house to house bringing the good news. They knock at every door and sing the Greek equivalent of carols: the *kalanda*. It is usually sung by boys to the accompaniment of small metal triangles and tiny clay drums, and the words go something like this:

Good evening, my lords; if it is your wish / of Christ's divine birth I shall tell the tale: / Christ is born today in the city of Bethlehem / the heavens are gladdened and all Creation rejoices / He lies in a manger among the horses / the King of Heaven and Maker of all things / a host of angels sing "Gloria in Excelsis" / and the shepherd's faith is worthy of heaven. / From Persia come three Kings bearing gifts / a bright star shows them the way, never failing.

The chief preparations for Christmas Eve center around the Christmas table. After several weeks of fasting, it is understandable that everyone, especially children, should grow joyfully impatient as the great day draws near. The Greeks do not use the Christmas tree as a symbol of the season. Instead, in nearly every home is a shallow bowl and there, hanging by a small wire looped over the rim, is a sprig of basil wound around a wooden cross. A small amount of water remains in the bowl to keep the basil alive and fresh. Each day the housewife takes the sprig-and-cross, dips it in water, and moves about the room sprinkling the special water everywhere as a means of keeping the *Killantzaroi* out of the house:

During the twelve-day period from Christmas to Epiphany, the Greeks believe the Killantzaroi make their appearance upon the earth. They are a species of goblins or sprites who appear only once a year; they are believed to emerge from the center of the earth. These creatures slip into people's houses through the chimney; they put out fires, ride astride people's backs, force them to dance, break dishes, and pester them in every way without causing any real harm.

147

Fear of the Killantzaroi gave rise to many protective measures that are interpreted today as Christmas customs. Burning an old shoe on the hearth is one, because the meaty odor of burning leather would drive them away. Hanging three pork bones inside the chimney is another. One of the most interesting customs is that of hanging a tuft of old flax over the door; by the time the Killantzaroi have finished untangling the flax and counting the threads, the cock crows and the sun scatters the darkness. Some people prefer to coax them away with sweets or honey cakes.

However, the principal means of keeping Killantzaroi away from the home is fire, which is generally believed to be unfavorable to sprites. The hearth is kept burning day and night throughout the Twelve Days. The Christmas log is placed in the grate and sprinkled with dried fruit. Often two logs are placed side by side and lit together because the ashes left will have more protective power. This is called "coupling of fire."

CHRISTMAS IN THE MIDDLE EAST

While the religions of the Middle East are predominantly Moslem and Hindu, there are a great many Christians who celebrate

Christmas, each in their own ways. English-speaking people observe the festival as an old-fashioned Christmas, while Christian natives combine Christian customs with those of their own country's religion. It was in Bethlehem where Christ was born and where members of all denominations assemble to sing carols in the Church of the Nativity on Christmas Eve.

Bethlehem. To Christians who dwell in Bethlehem, Christmas means the arrival of kinsfolk from far and near. They feast on cakes and home-pressed grapes from terraces below the town. Many Christian homes are denoted by a white cross painted over the door—a square one if the family is Greek Orthodox, a Latin one if it belongs to the Western branch of Christendom. In each home is a homemade crèche modeled after the original manger, and on a pole in the open square, a star is set up.

As of old, the Church of the Nativity is ablaze with flags and decorations on Christmas Eve. Men and women crowd the doorways, even the rooftops, to watch for the coming procession, which is dramatically heralded by a galloping horseman holding aloft a streaming banner. A corps of native police, mounted on fiery Arabian horses, is followed by a solitary horseman standing upon a coal-black steed, carrying the cross on high. Following and completing the procession are the cortege of churchmen and members of the government and their two-wheeled carriages with their picturesque Oriental jehus.

The procession solemnly enters the church. Because the placing of the ancient effigy of the Holy Child cannot be seen by the public, the people move forward in the church, pass behind the high altars, and down the steep, winding steps which lead to the grotto. Here, marked by a silver star, is the site of the birth of Jesus. Here, too, is the site of the manger where the Holy babe lay.

Iran. This country played an important part in the history of the first Chrstmas, for it was supposedly from there that the Three Wise Men came, the Magi who studied the stars. To boys and girls who are Greek Orthodox, the twenty-five days before Christmas are known as "Little Fast." "Big Fast" is six weeks before Easter, during which no meat, eggs, milk, or cheese is eaten. It is a time of peace and meditation.

Syria. Christmas Eve in Syria is spent in worship and prayer. In the evening a bonfire of vine stems is made in the middle of each church, in memory of the Magi, who were cold from their journey. Legend tells that a camel, the youngest of those bearing the Wise Men, fell down, exhausted by the journey. The Christ child blessed it and conferred immortality upon it. For this reason, the Syrian Santa Claus is the camel, who brings gifts to the children on New Years' Day. Before going to bed that night, little boys and girls set a bowl of water and wheat outside the house; in the morning, the good find gifts, and the naughty find a black mark on their wrists.

Old Armenia. On Christmas morning, a child is presented with an apple by his parents and friends. It is the custom to stick a coin or coins into the side of the apple. The children have a jolly time seeing who gets the most apples stuffed with precious coins. In another custom practiced at Christmas time, children climb up on housetops and lower a basket tied to the end of a long rope down the side of a wall, or down the chimney. The baskets are then filled with candy and often homemade gifts.

Iraq. Most people in Iraq are followers of Mohammed but there are sufficient numbers of Christians in cities to hold a Christmas celebration. One unusual ceremony held in courtyards on Christmas Eve combines the Nativity with Moslem customs used in celebrating their New Year's and other festivals.

A fire is lighted in one corner of the courtyard. One of the children reads the story of the Nativity from an Arabic Bible, while the other members of the family hold lighted candles. The bonfire is made of dried thorns, and the future of the house for the coming year depends upon the way the fire burns. If the thorns burn to ashes, the family will have good fortune. While the fire is burning a psalm is sung. When the fire is reduced to ashes, everyone jumps over them three times and makes a wish.

A charming custom takes place in the church on Christmas Day. A fire is built in the church, and while it burns, men chant a hymn. Then there is a procession in which the bishop carries an image of the Infant Jesus on a scarlet pillow. The service ends with the blessing of the people. The bishop reaches forth and touches a member of the congregation with his hand, putting his blessing upon him. That person touches the one next to him, and so on, until all have received "the Touch of Peace."

India. Because of international influence on her people, India has, perhaps, the most cosmopolitan Christmas in the world. Just to name a few: Christmas trees from Germany, ornaments from America, greeting cards from England, crèche from France, books from Greece.

Christmas is set against a background of scarlet poinsettia trees and tropical plants. Children in brightly colored dresses, accompanied by an orchestra of drums and cymbals, perform group dances, using gaily colored sticks as they do in their native dances. Gifts are exchanged, especially with children, and servants except *baksheesh*, which means coins. In turn, servants present a lemon to the head of the household on Christmas morning, a symbol of high esteem, bearing wishes for a long life and prosperity.

CHRISTMAS IN AFRICA

Wherever Christian missionaries have gone in Africa, Christmas is celebrated much as in the Western world. Also settlers in European colonies have clung to Old World customs which, in turn, have been adopted by Africans but with some of their own culture added. Gifted leaders have not only produced new music for this special occasion, but have added rhythm and chants to familiar carols that make them more meaningful to the people.

Ethiopa. In Addis Ababa, the capital city, Christmas begins at four in the morning, when church bells ring for early service. Later in the day, children dressed in their finest clothes walk to the royal palace to receive gifts from the Emperor.

Congo. Because Christmas is celebrated where it is warm and sunny, many people prepare a special dinner and place it on tables outside their houses. There they entertain invited friends or whoever comes along to share the joyful celebration.

In Christian churches, it is sometimes the custom to present a

151

"love offering" to the Child Jesus on His birthday. About nine or ten o'clock in the morning members gather to listen to the singing of carols by special musical groups. The most important part of the service is the "March Around Offering" in which everyone takes part. As the members march around the altar, each one lays his birthday gift on a raised platform which has been constructed for the purpose. Those without money will bring gifts they have made or some vegetable or fruit from their gardens or orchards.

South Africa. Christmas is a summer holiday in South Africa. It is a day of contradictions—the windows are draped with sparkling cotton wool and tinsel, yet it is an out-of-door day when people go to the beaches, the rivers, and shaded mountain slopes.

English-speaking children hang up their stockings, feeling certain Father Christmas will fill them with gifts and goodies. Carol singers make their rounds on Christmas Eve to celebrate "Carols by Candlelight." Children are fond of the age-old custom of producing pantomimes—for instance, "Babes in the Wood," founded on one of the oldest ballads in the English language. Boxing Day, on December 26, when boxes of food and clothing are given to the poor, is also observed as a holiday.

For the native African, Christmas Day is a day of good eating and a lively exchange and enjoyment of gifts. The festival is a carnival-like week of singing, dancing and feasting.

CHRISTMAS IN THE FAR EAST

Cities in the Far East, wherever American troops are stationed, are taken over completely by the commercial observance of Christmas. All stores and shops are elaborately decorated with tinsel and Christmas ornaments, carols are broadcast over loud speakers, and shoppers are eager to buy American goods. Decorated Christmas trees are not common, as the right type of tree (fir) is rare. Children call their tree the "Tree of Light" instead of a Christmas tree; it is decorated with brilliant paper flowers, colored paper chains, and papier-mâché stars.

Thailand. Any celebration of Christmas in Thailand is an institution of the church; it does not center around the home, as in

Western countries. Young people like to go caroling all night and it is their pleasure to awaken dignitaries such as a governor, a mayor, a bank manager, in the wee hours of the morning, and wish them a "Merry Christmas."

Japan. Christmas in Japan is much like it is in America, particularly in the cities. Tinsel and lights abound in dance halls, cafés, and pinball parlors where modern-minded Japanese go to celebrate. The department stores are filled with Christmas-tree decorations—colored balls, tinsel, angels—because most of these baubles are manufactured in Japan. Many Japanese try to do for others during the holidays. The hospitals, for instance, are decorated each with a Christmas tree, and children are chosen to sing carols to the patients. Sometimes they put on Nativity plays dealing with the flight of the Holy Family into Egypt, or stories of the shepherds and the Wise Men.

Philippine Islands. Filipino boys and girls proudly claim they have the longest Christmas in the world. For twenty-two lively days Christmas is celebrated, from December 16 to January 6. The festival begins at dawn on December 16 by pealing of the church bells, heralding the first of a novena of Masses. The service, at four in the morning, is called *Misa de Gallo* (since the Mass presumably starts as the first cock crows). Colorful wreaths and chains, made of brilliant tropical flowers, are worn by Filipino children as they take part in the festive after-Mass parade. A band leads the parade, providing the music for children's singing.

The Filipino children do not have a Christmas tree, but they decorate their homes with lavish care. Flags, bunting, palms, and many colorful flowers adorn their homes, and a candle is kept burning in the window all during the holidays. Hanging in front of every house is a large crepe-paper star, which is the most important part of the decoration.

Marshall Islands. The Stewardship Council, United Church of Christ, put on their "Christmas Tree," as they call it. A colorful Christmas tree is ingeniously hidden inside a wooden cross. As the men begin singing carols and hymns, the cross slowly opens and the tree rises from it. To make the opening more dramatic, the music is accompanied by noise of firecrackers which the singing group explode as they sing. Then the tree descends gently back into the cross as the carols are sung more softly and quietly. As the last carol ends, the two sides of the cross part and the tree remains, a Micronesian attempt to symbolize the birth, death, and resurrection of Christ.

Australia. "Carols by Candlelight," the world's biggest Christmas carol-singing festival, was born in Australia. On Christmas Eve, over twenty-five years ago, Norman Banks, radio announcer for Melbourne's 2 KZ Station, was hurrying homeward from the studio. Passing through a certain street, he heard a soft, quavering voice joining in the words of a carol sung over the radio. Peering through the window, he saw a little white-haired old lady, adding her gentle notes to the radio singer. To complete the Christmas effect, she was holding a lighted candle.

Somehow the scene made a deep impression on the radio announcer. He was inspired with the idea of getting all the inhabitants of Melbourne together on Christmas Eve, each person carrying a lighted candle, to join in the singing of carols. From the time the idea was launched, it is estimated that over a million persons have assembled for these "Carols by Candlelight" programs all over the world. A Carols by Candlelight Foundation was formed and the movement spread to New Zealand, then on to Johannesburg in South Africa, and to British Columbia and other parts of the world.

CENTRAL AMERICA

Central America greets Christmas with weather like midsummer. December is a season of bright flowers and ripe fruits. On Christmas Eve people stroll along the streets where there are many things to buy, such as candles, pictures of the Nativity, drinks, toys, and holiday foods. The music of guitars, castanets, and gourds fills the air. Suddenly, when the church bell calls, the streets are deserted, since all go inside to Midnight Mass.

Sometimes little processions are formed by two people carrying a manger, followed by gaily costumed children singing Christmas carols. The day of exchanging gifts is not Christmas but January 6 (Twelfth Night), when traditionally the Wise Men brought their gifts to Jesus.

Mexico. Christmas celebrations in Mexico begin on December 16 and end on Christmas Eve. Their chief feature is the *posada* ("lodging") in which people of the city or town enact the story of the search of Mary and Joseph for lodging. Each evening friends and relatives go in candlelit procession to some home. They carry figures of Mary and Joseph, and upon reaching the

155

door, ask in song for lodging, to be refused at first by the man of the house, but finally admitted with great rejoicing. Upon entering they kneel at the manger, which is found in every home, then spend the rest of the evening in fun—dancing, singing, breaking the high-swung *pinata* (a clay container in grotesque and highly decorated shape, filled with sweets and broken with the sticks held by blindfolded children).

Nicaragua. In Nicaragua, like most Latin America countries, the people retain many customs of Old Spain. Before the end of November, children begin to throng the streets, carrying fragrant bouquets for the altar of the Virgin and singing carols to the Queen of Heaven. On January 6, the Three Wise Men will bring gifts and then there will be fireworks.

SOUTH AMERICA

Christmas in South America continues to have a religious tone. Common to most people is the *presepio* ("the manger") and the *Missa do Gallo* ("Midnight Christmas Eve Mass") followed by singing of carols. Christmas dinner may be served outside under the shade of a tree, a trellis, or a veranda. A roast suckling pig is the favorite meat of the season.

In many South American countries there is a variation of the presepio known as the *protal* or *pesebre*. Instead of a manger scene under a tree or in a corner of a room, a whole room is filled with a landscape with tiny figures made to scale. It represents an entire region with mountains, hills, plains, and valleys. The central point is a replica of the manger at Bethlehem—but out on the hills are the shepherds overcome with the heavenly vision and Wise Men crossing the desert on their camels. The more elaborate ones include water mills, grottos, electric trains, while sailboats ply the waters of the sea.

Brazil. Since Christmas falls in midsummer weather, a colorful altar is often set up in the cathedral courtyard where the worshippers attend the Midnight Mass in a fiesta atmosphere of banners and religious trappings. Masses are especially popular at Christmas because the poorer people have no gifts or tree at home. Dances and fireworks fill the holidays, and afternoons are passed with picnics, swimming, and other diversions.

Columbia. Christmas Eve is the night of the *aguinalsos,* or "presents," when everyone disguises himself with fancy dress and mask and goes to make merry in the streets. But merrymaking and masquerade have a definite plan too. The idea is that everyone tries to recognize a friend in spite of the disguise, and when someone's identity is discovered, the discerning person claims an *aguinaldo,* or a gift from the one he recognizes. This jolly custom is especially popular with the young people, and above all with sweethearts, for the disguises are kept secret and each tries to outwit the other and be the first to win the *aguinaldo.*

INDEX

Adonis gardens, 7-8
Advent, 127-134
    in Europe, 128-133
Africa, ceremonies in, 123
    Christmas in, 151-152
    New Year's in, 15
Alaska, Christmas in, 143-144
    Iceworm "Winter Wonderland" Festival in, 31-32
All Fool's Day, 75
Alm trees, 87
American Indians, 125-126
Annapolis Valley Festival, Canada, 89
Arab countries, Epiphany in, 23
    (See also Middle East)
Arbor Day, 86-87
Armenia, Assumption Day in, 109
    Christmas in, 150
Armenian church, Candlemas in, 28
Ash Wednesday, 45, 47, 52, 61-62
Assumption Day, 109-110
Audubon societies, 93
Australia, Christmas in, 154-155
Austria, Corpus Christi in, 69
    Epiphany in, 21
    wine festival in, 121-122
Avani Mulam (Hindu), 107-109

Baby's first haircut, Peru, 39-40
Basil, St., 4
Belgium, Assumption Day in, 109
    Christmas in, 141
    Good Friday in, 54
    Great Gilles Carnival in, 34

May Day in, 85
St. Peter's Day in, 102
Shrimp Festival in, 105
Whitsunday in, 65-66
Bethlehem, Christmas in, 149
Bettara-Ichi (Sticky-Sticky Fair), Japan, 114-115
Bird Week, in Japan, 94-95
    in the United States, 93-94
Birthday trees, 86
Birthdays, in Vietnam, 13-14
Blessing of the Waters, 22
Blossom festivals, in Canada, 89
    in Holland, 90-91
    in Japan, 89-90
    in the United States, 88-89
Bolivia, Alacitas celebration in, 17
Book-reading Week, Japan, 115
Brazil, carnival in, 40-42
    Christmas in, 156-157
    New Year's Eve in, 17
    St. John's Day in, 101
Buddha, birthday of, 76-78
Buddhists, 11

Canada, blossom festival in, 89
    Halloween in, 119
    St. John's Day in, 100
Candlemas, 28-29
Carnivals, 32
    in Europe, 33-36
    in Mexico, 36-37
    in South America, 37-42
    in the United States, 32-33

159

in the Virgin Islands, 36
Cheese Week, Greece, 35
Children's Day, Turkey, 80-81
China, Buddha's birthday in, 78
    Ching Ming in, 87
    Ch'u Yuan in, 103-104
    Li Ch'un in, 91
    New Year's in, 1, 9-11
    star festival in, 25-26
Ching Ming, China, 87
Christmas, 135-157
    in Africa, 151-152
    in Central America, 155-156
    in Europe, 138-148
    in the Far East, 152-154
    and gift giving, 135-137
    in the Middle East, 148-151
    in South America, 156-157
    in the United States, 137
Christmas cookies, 140
Christmas crib, 143-144
Christmas customs, 140-143
Christmas decorations, 139
Christmas markets, 128-129
Christmas trees, 139
Ch'u Yuan (Dragon Boat Festival),
    China, 103-104
Colombia, Christmas in, 157
Congo, the, Christmas in, 151-152
Cormorant fishing, Japan, 94-95
Corpus Christi, 67-68
    in Europe, 68-70
    in Mexico, 70
    in the United States, 68
Cross of Petition, 17-18
Czechoslovakia, Palm Sunday in, 49

Day of Holy Cross, Mexico, 93
Day of Ste Lucia, 132-133
Day of Youth, Yugoslavia, 75
Denmark, Christmas in, 139, 141
    New Year's in, 3
    St. John's Day in, 101
Doll Festival, Japan, 72

Easter, 38-62
    in Africa, 62
    food for, 61-62
    sunrise services on, 59
Easter parades, 59-60

Easter rabbit, 60
Egypt, Epiphany in, 23
    Sham Al-Nessim in, 74-75
Eighth Moon festivals, China, 115-118
Elevation of the Cross (Holy Cross),
    113-114
England (see Great Britain)
Epiphany, 19-20
    Eastern legends of, 23-24
    in Europe, 21-23
    in the Middle East, 23-24
    in the United States, 20-21
Episcopal church, 57
Equador, Old Year in, 16-17
Estonia, St. John's Day in, 99
Ethiopia, Christmas in, 151
Europe, Candlemas in, 28-29
    carnivals in, 32-33
    Christmas in, 138-148
    Corpus Christi in, 68-70
    Epiphany in, 21-23
    Groundhog Day in, 29
    May Day celebrations in, 84-85
    New Year's in, 1, 3-5
    Shrove Tuesday in, 44
    summer festivals in, 99, 105-106, 109-
    110

Fall festivals, 112-126
    in China, 115-118
    in Europe, 119-122
    in Japan, 114-115
    Moslem, 112-113
    in the United States, 119-120, 124-
    126
Far East, New Year's in, 9-11
    (See also names of countries, as
    Japan)
Feast of Esther, 43
Feast of the Immaculate Conception,
    131-132
Festival of Lanterns, China, 9-10
Fiesta del Grillo (the cricket), Italy,
    105
Finland, Lapp Lady Day in, 62
    St. Peter's Day in, 103
Fire Festival, India, 8
First Fruits of the Alps, Switzerland,
    105-106
France, carnival in, 33-34

160

Christmas in, 143, 145
Corpus Christi in, 68
May Day in, 85
Fuji, Mt., 110

Gayatrijapam, India, 106-107
Germany, Advent in, 128-129
Christmas in, 141
Epiphany in, 21
New Year's in, 3-4
St. Martin's Day in, 122-123
tree planting in, 87
Whitsuntide in, 65
Gloucester (Mass.), 102
Good Friday, 45, 53-54
in Spain, 54-55
Great Britain, All Fool's Day in, 75
Corpus Christi in, 69-70
Groundhog Day in, 29
Guy Fawkes Day in, 120-121
May Day in, 85
Mothering Sunday in, 47-48
St. George's Day in, 82
Whitsunday in, 67
Greece, Cheese Week in, 35-36
Christmas in, 146-148
Epiphany in, 22-23
Lenten calendar in, 46-47
New Year's in, 4-5
Palm Sunday in, 50
Procession of the Swallows in, 71-72
St. George's Day in, 82
St. John's Day in, 99-100
St. Menas' Day in, 124
St. Nicholas' Day in, 130-131
Whitsunday in, 66
Greek Orthodox Church, 4, 46, 113, 142
Holy Week in, 56-57
Groundhog Day, 29-30
Guy Fawkes Day, England, 120-121

Haft-sin, 7-8
Halloween, 119-120
Hamish Asar Bishvat (New Year of
Trees), 18
Hana Matsuri (birth of Buddha), Japan,
76-78
Hanoi, 12
Hanukka, 134
Harvest festivals, 118-119

Hawaii, Narcissus Festival in, 26-27
Hindus, 1, 8, 91, 48
summer festivals among, 106-109
Holi (Fire Festival), India, 8
Holland, Christmas in, 141
May Day in, 85
Tulip Festival in, 90-91
Whitsunday in, 65-66
Hollywood Bowl, sunrise service in, 59
Holy Saturday, 55-56
Holy Week, 51-57
in Greek Orthodox Church, 56-57
among Protestants, 57
Horoscopes, 13-14
Hot cross buns, 61
Hurricane Thanksgiving, Virgin Islands,
125

Iceworm "Winter Wonderland" Festi-
val, Alaska, 31-32
India, Christmas in, 151
Gayatrijapam in, 106-107
Masi Magham in, 91-92
New Year's in, 1, 8-9
International Women's Day, 73
Iran, Christmas in, 149-150
New Year's in, 7-8
Iraq, Christmas in, 151-152
Ireland, Halloween in, 119
harvest festival in, 118
St. Patrick's Day in, 74
Islam holidays, principal, 79-80
Israel, New Year of Trees in, 18
Italy, Assumption Day in, 109
carnival in, 35
Christmas in, 143, 146
Corpus Christi in, 68-69
Day of Ste Lucia in, 133
Fiesta del Grillo in, 105
New Year's in, 3
St. Peter's Day in, 102-103

Janus Befors, 1
Japan, Bird Week in, 94
cherry viewing in, 89-90
Christmas in, 153-154
cormorant fishing in, 94-95
Doll Festival in, 72
fall festivals in, 114-115

161

Hana Matsuri (Flower Festival) in, 76-78
Imperial Poem-reading Ceremony in, 27-28
kite flying in, 93
May Day in, 84
mountain climbing in, 110
New Year's in, 14-15
night-singing insects in, 105
shellfish gathering in, 76
Time-Observance Day in, 97-98
Jews, and Hanukkah, 134
    and New Year of Trees, 18
    New Year's celebration by, 1-2, 5-7
    and Passover, 63-64
    and Purim, 42-43
    and Shavuot, 70-71
    and Sukkot, 118, 123-124
Julius Caesar, 1

Kiddush, the, 6
Kite Day, China, 117-118
Kite flying, Japan, 93
Kneeling Sunday, 66
Koran, the, 7-8

Laetare Sunday, 48
Lailat-al-Quade (Night of Destiny), Arab countries, 23
Lapp Lady Day, 62
Lazybones, 66
Lebanon, 24
Lent, 45-50
Lenten calendars, ancient, 46-47
Li Ch'un (spring ox), China, 91
Lima, Peru, 95-96
Luther, Martin, 122-123

Magi, the, 19-21
Maharram (Muslim New Year), 9
Marseille, France, Christmas market in, 128-129
Marshall Islands, Christmas in, 154
Masi Magham, India, 91-92
Maundy Thursday, 53
May baskets, 85-86
May Day celebrations, 84-86
Merchant's Flower Market, Haarlem, 65-66
Mexico, All Fool's Day in, 75

Candlemas in, 28-29
Christmas in, 155-156
Corpus Christi in, 69
Day of Holy Cross in, 93
New Year's in, 17-18
Palm Sunday in, 49-50
St. John's Day in, 101
St. Martin's Carnival in, 36-37
Middle East, Christmas in, 148-151
    Epiphany in, 23-24
    New Year's in, 5-8
    (See also Arab countries)
Midnight Mass, 155-156
Milagrous, Señor de los, 95
Missouri, Groundhog Day in, 30
Mohammed, birthday of, 79
Moon cakes, 116-117
Moon Hare, 117
Moon worship, 116
Morton, J. Sterling, 86
Moslems, 112-113, 148
Mothering Sunday, 47-48
Mountain climbing, Japan, 110
Muslim New Year, 9

Narcissus Festival, Hawaii, 26-27
Near East, New Year's in, 1
Nebraska, 86
Netherlands (see Holland)
New Orleans, Mardi Gras in, 32-33
New Year's, as day of reconciliation, 2
    food for, 5, 8
    around the world, 1-18
Nicaragua, Christmas in, 156
Nice, France, carnival in, 33-34
Night-singing insects, Japan, 105
No-Ruz (Iran's New Year), 7-8
Norway, Christmas in, 138, 140
    New Year's in, 3
Nuremberg, Christmas market in, 129

Oberammergau, New Year's in, 4
Oshoogatsu (Japanese New Year), 14

Palestine, 87
Palm Sunday, 49-50
    in Africa, 62
    in Rome, 50
Parade of the Months, Italy, 35
Passover, 63-64

162

Pee-Mai (New Year's festival), Thailand, 11-12
Peking, New Year's in, 10
Pennsylvania, Groundhog Day in, 30
Peru, baby's first haircut in, 39-40
  fiestas in, 111
  purple spring in, 95-96
  Water-Throwing Carnival in, 37-38
  Zafa-casa in, 38-39
Philippines, the, Advent in, 131-132
  Christmas in, 144, 154
  May Day in, 84
Poland, Christmas in, 142
Pope, the, 48, 50
Portugal, carnival in, 34-35
  Corpus Christi in, 68
  New Year's in, 3, 5
  St. Peter's Day in, 102
Pretzels, 61-62
Procession of the Giants, France and Belgium, 65
Procession of the Swallows, Greece, 71-72
Promenades of Santo Domingo and San Francisco, Peru, 111
Protestants, 122
  and Holy Week, 54, 57
  and Lent, 47, 49
Purim, 42-43
Purple spring, Peru, 95-96

Ramadan, Fast of (Moslem), 112-113
Réveillon, France, 145
Rio de Janeiro, carnival in, 40-42
Roman Catholics, 45, 101-102, 113
  and Christmas, 143-146
  and Holy Week, 51-56
Romania, Christmas in, 142
Romans, the, 1
Rome, Palm Sunday in, 50
Rosh Hashana, 1, 5-6
Russia, Christmas in, 142
  International Women's Day in, 73
  May Day in, 83
  St. George's Day in, 83
Ryan, W. A., 88

Saigon, 12
St. George's Day, 81-83
St. John's Day, 98-101

St. Martin's Carnival, Mexico, 36-37
St. Martin's Day, 121-123
St. Menas' Day, Greece, 124
St. Nicholas' Day, 129-131
St. Patrick's Day, 73-74
St. Peter's Day, 101-103
Salzillo, 55
Scandinavia, Christmas in, 138-141
  St. John's Day in, 99
  (See also names of countries, as Norway)
Scotland, All Fool's Day in, 75
Seville, Good Friday in, 55
Sham Al-Nessim (The Smelling of Spring), Egypt, 74-75
Shavuot (Feast of Weeks), 70-71
Shellfish gathering, Japan, 76
Shenandoah Valley Festival, 88-89
Shrimp Festival, Belgium, 105
Shrove Tuesday, 43-44
Sierra Leone, New Year's in, 15
"Singing in the May," England, 85
Smoke money, 67
Songkran (Buddhist New Year's), 11
South Africa, Christmas in, 152
South America, carnivals in, 37-42
  Christmas in, 156-157
  New Year's in, 16-17
  summer festivals in, 95-96, 111
Spain, Assumption Day in, 109
  carnival in, 34-35
  Christmas in, 143, 145-146
  Corpus Christi in, 68
  Epiphany in, 21
  New Year's in, 5
Spring festivals, early, 63-83
  late, 84-96
Star festival, China, 25-26
Star of Seven, German, 128
Stations of the Cross, 54
Sukkot, 118, 123-124
Summer festivals, 97-111
  in Asia, 106-109
  in Canada, 100
  in Europe, 99, 105-106, 109-110
  in Japan, 97-98, 105
  in South America, 95-96, 111
  in the United States, 102
Sunrise services, 59
Sweden, Christmas in, 138, 140-141

163

Day of Ste Lucia in, 132-133
Epiphany in, 21
Switzerland, Christmas in, 142-143
Epiphany in, 21
First Fruits of the Alps in, 105-106
May Day in, 85
Syria, 24
Christmas in, 150
St. George's Day in, 83-84

Tel Aviv, Hanukkah in, 134
Tenchi, Emperor, 97
Tet (Vietnam New Year), 12-13
Thailand, Christmas in, 152-153
New Year's in, 11-12
Three Hour Service, 53-54
Three Masses, the, 143
Three Wise Men, the, 19-20
Time-Observance Day, Japan, 97-98
Tito, Marshal, birthday of, 75
Tree planting ceremonies, 86-87
Tulip Festival, Holland, 90-91
Turkey, Children's Day in, 80-81
T'wan Yüan Chieh (Festival of Re-
union), China, 115-116
Twelfth Night (see Epiphany)

UNICEF, 119-120
United States, Arbor Day in, 86-87
blossom festivals in, 88-89
carnivals in, 32-33
Christmas in, 137
Corpus Christi in, 68
Epiphany in, 20-21

Groundhog Day in, 29-30
Halloween in, 119-120
May Day in, 85-86
New Year's in, 1-3
St. George's Day in, 82
St. Peter's Day in, 102
summer festivals in, 88-89
Thanksgiving in, 124-126

Valentine's Day, 30-31
Vietnam, birthdays in, 13-14
New Year's in, 1, 12-13
Virgin Islands, carnival in, 36
Hurricane Thanksgiving in, 125
Whitsunday in, 65

Water Festival, Thailand, 11
Water-throwing carnival, Peru, 37-38
Wellesley College, May Day at, 86
Wenatchee Valley Festival, 89
Whitsuntide, 64-66
Wine festivals, Austria, 121-122
Winter festivals, 25-44
World Day of Prayer, 47

Yom Kippur, 1, 5-7
Yuan Tan (Chinese New Year), 9
Yugoslavia, Day of Youth in, 75
Yule men, 138-139

Zapa-casa (Finishing of the House),
Peru, 38-39
Zoroastrians, 7